Sarah Johnson Prichard

The Old Stone Chimney

Sarah Johnson Prichard

The Old Stone Chimney

ISBN/EAN: 9783743346628

Manufactured in Europe, USA, Canada, Australia, Japa

Cover: Foto ©ninafisch / pixelio.de

Manufactured and distributed by brebook publishing software (www.brebook.com)

Sarah Johnson Prichard

The Old Stone Chimney

THE OLD STONE CHIMNEY.

THE

OLD STONE CHIMNEY.

BY

S. J. PRITCHARD,

AUTHOR OF

"MARTHA'S HOOKS AND EYES," "KATE MORGAN'S SOLDIERS," "KENNY CARLE'S UNIFORM," "JOE AND JIM," Etc.

NEW YORK:
ANSON D. F. RANDOLPH & CO.,
900 BROADWAY.

Books by Cousin Kate.
(Catharine D. Bell.)

"Written with taste, skill, and effect. Books that please while they profit every pure-minded reader."

Hope Campbell. 16mo. Cloth, $1.25.
Horace and May. 16mo. Cloth, $1.25.
Kenneth and Hugh. 16mo. Cloth, $1.25.
Lily Gordon. 16mo. Cloth, $1.25.
Rest and Unrest. 16mo. Cloth, $1.25.
Sydney Stuart. 16mo. Cloth, $1.25.

Anson D. F. Randolph & Company,
900 Broadway, Cor. 20th St., New York.

Either or all of the above mailed post free, on receipt of price affixed. Fractional amounts can be remitted in postage-stamps.

THE OLD STONE CHIMNEY

Chapter One.

BIRMINGHAM is the name of a village in the town of Derby, in Connecticut. The Housatonic River separates forever the old town from the new village, and the little fiery river of the Naugatuck valley does its utmost to widen the distance between the two, for it work its willful way out from the hills, and pours its waters, weary with their work of turning many mill-wheels, into the broad peaceful flow of the Housatonic, and together the rivers roll on, to pour themselves at last into the waters of Long Island Sound.

One May-day a group of boys were at play in Birmingham.

"Where did you get it, Dick?" asked one.

"Oh! up in the woods a piece." "One, two, three, four!" said Dick; "now try it."

Four boys were kneeling on the pavement, around a turtle that Dick Jones had captured. The poor thing did not like its captivity, and was doing its utmost to escape, but every avenue was cut off by fire and smoke.

A box of matches lay on the stones, and at the instant Dick Jones reached the number of four in his counting, Albert Elder drew a match on the pavement, and held it close to the turtle's head. It drew back, evidently suffering pain. A moment more, and another torturing match was alight, and held close to the turtle's head. Whatever way it turned in its agony, the same fate awaited it.

A footstep was heard approaching, and one of the boys turned to see who it might be.

"Look here, boys! that's Thode Day; he won't like our sport; let's hide," said Dick Jones, catching up the turtle and retreating with it behind a high and tight board fence.

The object of their torture showed every sign of suffering that its poor dumb nature could show, but it failed to call forth the slightest feeling of sympathy or kindness.

No sooner had Theodore Day passed out of sight, than the four boys returned to their cruel amusement. The day was one of spring's fairest and brightest. The buds on the trees were opening out their store, and shaking their emerald banners to the breeze.

Full of happiness, and rejoicing in every thing about her, little Lulu Day was on her way from school, and chanced to pass by the boys who were torturing the turtle with burning matches.

Lulu came upon them so suddenly, that they had no time to run and hide, as they had from her brother Theodore.

She stood still as soon as she saw the turtle.

Dick Jones held a match in his hand. The pavement was strewn with burned fragments, that told Lulu the story. A quick look of horror passed over her face, and then one of sympathy.

"Dick, won't you give me that turtle, please?" Lulu asked.

"Indeed I won't, it's my turtle, I found it in the woods."

"I know, but I want it very much indeed, Dick. Dick! *don't* torture it so!" she cried, as the wicked boy drew a match, and held it close to the head, drawn as far back into the shell as it was possible.

"O Lulu Day! *you* needn't mind, it don't hurt you one bit; and it's such fun to see it snap," said Alfred Elder, "look here! quick now!" and a flaming match was thrust under the shell.

Lulu Day darted forward and caught up the turtle in her hand, before the boys were aware of her intention. Her first impulse was to run away with it, but the thought came, " It is not mine," and she stood still.

The turtle was stupefied with the fumes of the burning matches, and did not stir.

" Lulu Day, give that turtle to me this minute. I would think *you'd* know better than to steal; your father preaches enough; he'd better teach his own children first," said Dick Jones, getting up from the pavement and going to Lulu.

Without a word, the little girl

stooped, and laid the animal gently upon the flagging at her feet. She secretly wished that it had wings wherewith to fly away, but she said: " Dick Jones, won't you please to promise me that no one shall touch this poor hurt thing, until I come back? I won't be gone but five minutes."

"You needn't go after Thode, for you won't find him," said Dick, who was secretly afraid of Lulu's brother.

" No, I did not think of my brother. I will come back, if you'll only promise me."

Dick hesitated, but Arthur whispered, " Promise!" and two or three who had joined the group, urged him by glances to acquiesce.

" Go on then, I'll let it lie there," he said.

"And no one shall burn a match, or touch it, you promise?" questioned Lulu.

"I'll stand guard — never fear."

Lulu sped away as if life depended upon the fleetness of her movements.

She reached her home, and leaving gate and doors widely open, she rushed up to her father's study, a place that she was forbidden to enter uncalled.

Her heart knocked almost as loudly as did her hand on the door. Obeying the summons to enter, the little girl stood before her father.

"What is it, Lulu? Did your mother send you here?"

"No, papa, I came; won't you please to give me some money very quick, just this very minute, for some wicked boys are killing a turtle that they found in the woods. They are putting burning matches right into its face and eyes, and it's most dead," and Lulu's tears followed her words.

"Where are they?" asked Mr. Day.

"Oh! they're on the street! Quick, papa; they promised not to touch it until I got back."

"Do you think they will sell it to you?"

"Oh! yes, for money! and I won't ask you for any again in a long, long time."

Lulu Day seized the dime fresh from the mint, out of her father's hand, and forgetting doors in her haste, she ran to the street, and the tormented turtle. There it lay on the pavement, just as she had left it.

"Your time is up," cried Dick, and

just before Lulu reached the place, he stooped and drew a match. He held it in his hand, just ready to apply to his victim, when Lulu seized the hand, and put something in it. The something was the shining dime.

"There, Dick Jones, that is yours, if you will give me this turtle. I want it; see, it's pretty."

For a moment Dick hesitated. The bribe in his hand was a temptation, so was the means of tormenting any thing or any body; for the law of loving-kindness was unknown to the boy.

Lulu looked so much in earnest, and held the torpid animal so lovingly, that Albert Elder's heart was won over to her cause, and he whispered in Dick's ear: "You know you can buy the marbles you wanted with that dime."

"So I can, it comes just in time; you can have the creature if you want it, but it will die, I know," said Dick.

"Oh! I thank you," said Lulu, and now that the property was her own, and the victim safe from farther persecution, she said: "How do you know, boys, but you will get terribly punished for treating any thing so cruelly? I know one thing; if I was God, I'd do something to make you feel sorry. You are awfully wicked, every one of you, to hurt a poor thing like this!" And Lulu stroked the hard shell, as if it would soothe the hurt that it had received.

The four boys who had been engaged in the transaction, felt the power of Lulu's sermon, notwithstanding the anger that attended its delivery, and they went away whistling with all their power, to drown the voice of conscience, that whispered to each one of them.

Lulu carried her turtle home. It was not until hours had gone by, that life returned to it. Then it began to thrust forth its head, and return it to the shell, as if in great agony from the burns it had received.

Lulu watched it carefully; she fed it, and did her utmost to make it comfortable. She put it away for the night in a place of safety as she thought, and very early in the morning went out to look for it. To her astonishment it was not to be found. She enlisted Theodore's sympathies in her behalf, and the two searched carefully the premises, but were compelled to think that it had escaped.

Now, it so happened, that the turtle, by the time of morning, had recovered from the pain of the burns, sufficiently to think of its home in the forest and by the river banks; and it escaped from its prison, and would have found its way to its old haunts, but for two boys.

The two boys were Albert and Dick. They were on their way to a tract of pasture-land, and were driving cows there; when, in passing Mr. Day's house, they espied the turtle just as he was leaving the premises.

Dick made a prisoner of it without the slightest hesitation. He dropped it into a basket that he carried, and went on.

"What are you going to do with that turtle?" said Albert.

"Do with it? Why, keep it, of course. Isn't it mine? When I found it the first time, it was mine, and why not now, pray?" said Dick.

"Well, you *are* the meanest boy in all Birmingham, to sell a thing one day, and pick it up and claim it the next. I tell you what, Dick Jones, that sermon that Lulu Day gave us yesterday is enough for me; you don't catch me in such mean business again very soon."

"Before I'd care what kind of a sermon Lulu Day preached, or any body else. I tell you this turtle is mine, and I'm going to keep it too, and won't we have fun about the time the young lady takes her walk home from school to-morrow night!"

"No, I will have nothing to do with it, and I won't be seen in your company again, not even driving cows with you." And Albert Elder cried out to the cows under his charge to "keep to the right, and let Dick Jones pass by."

Dick was very angry, but he said nothing, and as went on he was devising some plan of revenge, some way in which he could punish Albert Elder for deserting him.

The cows were driven upon their pasture meadows, which adjoined.

Dick had some trouble in replacing the bars. He could not put them in order alone, and he put down his bas ket and called to Albert, who was half-way down the hill.

Albert went back and gave all the assistance that was needed cheerfully, and without one sign of unwillingness.

The turtle took his opportunity to escape, doubtless thinking it his only chance. He had hidden in the stone wall; but, either not being an intelligent turtle, or not appreciating his advantage, he did not remain concealed, and so was put into the basket again, and taken by Dick Jones to a place of safety.

The afternoon of the same day, Lulu was going home, when she encountered Dick.

"Look here, Miss Day!" he called "I've something to show you," and Dick uncovered the basket he carried.

"Wasn't I lucky to find another turtle just like yours?" he asked.

"Where did you get it?" questioned Lulu.

"Oh! I found it on my way to drive the cows this morning."

"In the road?"

"No, up by the high stone wall. I don't care now if you have got mine."

"But I have not. It got away and jumped off in the night, I suppose, for this morning I could not find it, and Thole and I looked everywhere. How do you know but *this* one is mine?"

"How could it get upon the stone wall a mile and a half away, I should like to know?" asked Dick.

"I should know in a minute, 'cause

I tied a bit of red sewing-silk around one of its legs. Please let me look," said Lulu. Dick Jones held the turtle out of her reach and ran off.

The little girl was in great distress. She knew not what to do, and in the midst of her fear, her brother Theodore appeared.

"O good Thody! I never was so glad to see you in my life. That bad boy, Dick Jones, has got a turtle, and he won't let me see whether it is mine or not; and you know I tied a piece of sewing-silk around it. Won't you make him let you see it?"

In an instant Theodore was in rapid pursuit of Dick Jones, who was compelled to flee so fast that he hadn't time to take off the silk, which he was very anxious to do.

Theodore came upon him, caught the basket out of his hand, and before the boy could resist in the least, Theodore was in possession of the turtle.

There was the mark, Lulu's mark upon it, and without ceremony Theodore returned it to its lawful owner.

Great was Lulu's delight. She carried it home in triumph, determined that it should be guarded so carefully that it should never more escape.

"Papa, how I do wish somebody would burn matches right under that horrid boy's nose!" exclaimed Lulu, her voice shaking and her little person all athrob with anger, as she carried her pet into her father's presence to show him where Dick Jones had fastened pins into the much-suffering turtle.

They were carefully drawn out before Mr. Day spoke to Lulu.

"Poor little thing, to be so abused!" murmured Lulu softly, as the last pin was removed; and then as the wrongs that had been perpetrated rushed into her mind, she suddenly exclaimed: "I wish I was big and strong, and wasn't afraid of Dick Jones, I know what I'd do."

"Well, Lulu, what would you do?"

"I'd catch him, and tie him fast to a tree, and put these pins into him until he'd promise to behave better."

"O my child!"

"But I would, papa, and then he'd know just how much it hurt, and now he thinks it is nice, just because the turtle jumps about and looks funny, and he don't feel it himself."

"And then Dick Jones's mother, if he has one, would hear that Lulu Day had fastened her boy to a tree and pricked him with pins, and she would think that the little girl who could do such a wicked thing ought to be punished for it, and, being very angry with her, she would devise some way of making her feel pins and needles; and then I should be very angry, and go about to punish somebody else, and at last the whole neighborhood would be at war and Derby and Birmingham, perhaps, would throw hot stones at each other across the river."

"O papa! how funny you make it all. See, the turtle aches, I know i does, it wriggles so."

"The poor thing does suffer, I know, and am very much pained that boys can be so cruel; but I wished to show you that God can punish sin better than we can. We, in our attempts, make the trouble greater by spreading it; whereas, if we only wait, God will scarcely show to us a wiser way, for He is just to all the creatures that He has made."

"And will He punish Dick Jones?" asked Lulu.

"He surely will, in His own way and time."

"Good! then I can wait, papa, and I won't carry a single pin with me on the street;" and to put away temptation, Lulu drew forth a pin from her dress and laid it upon the table.

"Then you wish Dick Jones to be made to suffer?"

"To be sure, papa, because you say

it is right; and if God punishes him, it must be right that he should be hurt, and don't you think I ought to be glad?"

"No, Lulu, I do not; I think you should be sorry, and ask God to forgive Dick Jones, and give him a kind heart, that he may be tender and true toward every thing that is weaker than he is."

The turtle gave signs of great pain, thrusting forth its burned head as far as it could, and then suddenly retreating into its shell.

Lulu's eyes filled with tears of pity. "O papa! how can I?" she asked. She stooped down, and stroked the turtle as if she would soothe its pain. "Papa, it doesn't move any more; do you think it can be going to die?"

Mr. Day took it up. It neither moved nor gave signs of life.

"It will not suffer any more, Lulu; it is dead."

"Give it to me, please, papa; may be it isn't quite dead."

Lulu sat down upon the carpet with the turtle in her apron, and watched it carefully for a full half-hour, and all the while tears were falling upon the shell, tears of pity, mingled with indignation. At last she put it down, and went to her father's side.

In a moment his occupation was left for her.

"What is it, my dear?"

"I shouldn't like to see Dick Jones die as my poor turtle did, if I was his sister, and may be he has one."

"I am thankful to hear you say so,

Now that the turtle is dead and can suffer no more, can you ask God to forgive Dick Jones?"

"Yes, papa, I can, for I am sorry for his mother, and I suppose she loves him. I'll pray to God to forgive him for her sake, and that she needn't feel bad."

"Lulu, I will tell you for whose sake all our prayers must go up to heaven. Christ loved every one who lived on the earth so much that He came down and was nailed to the cross with nails in His hands and His feet, that they might be forgiven by His Father. He loves us better than father or mother——"

Lulu interrupted her father to ask: "And would Christ feel badly to have Dick punished?"

"Yes. He does not like to have His children suffer, not even for their sins."

"Then I must ask God to forgive Dick Jones for Christ's sake, because Christ loves him, must I, papa?"

"Yes, Lulu."

Lulu kneeled down, and for a moment the room was very still. Up through the silence went Lulu's prayer: "Please, Father in heaven, to forgive Dick Jones for burning the turtle, and putting pins into it, for Christ's sake." And then Lulu took up the dead turtle, and went and hid it in the grass.

Chapter Two.

LULU DAY had not spoken to Dick Jones until the afternoon, when the turtle called forth her sympathy and her words. She had oftentimes seen him at play on the street, but knew no more of him than his name indicated.

Dick Jones was the son of a laborer in one of the iron-mills in Birmingham. Mr. Jones worked, because it was his habit to work. He left a large share of his earnings at a grocery in the village, or at a public house across the river, from the same cause. He left his wife to pass her evenings alone, and his children to wander in the street, because he had formed the habit of doing so. His days were very much alike, except that the rolling-mill was closed on Sundays, and he could not work. He was indifferent to every thing about him. You could not see the man passing through the street, without feeling that he was asleep, and that a strong, thorough shaking would be to him a kindness; but no stirring event had come as yet into his life.

Mrs. Jones was a quiet, long-suffering little woman, into whose mind it rarely came to question any thing, although she did sometimes wonder why her children should not be like other children; but since they were not, she tried to be reconciled to her lot. And as they grew older, they passed more and more from under her control; and if, at times, when some great act of rebellion startled her, she thought of the future and its coming events, she as quickly turned to the fact, that she could not help it, and it was of no use to worry about it.

A deep lethargy had fallen upon the household. To their spiritual and temporal interest they were alike indifferent.

Albert Elder's mother was a widow. She lived across the Housatonic River, on a small farm that had been her husband's; and Albert and Fanny were her children.

The influence of Albert Elder's home was good and kindly, but the boy was astray. During the winter, he had devoted too much of his time to the companionship of idle boys, either on the river, when King Cold held it in his icy clasp, or upon the high hills that were snow-covered; and he found it very hard to overcome the habit. Naturally Albert Elder was a kind boy; but at the time of the incident recorded in the first chapter, he was fast becoming a slave to the evil influences that surrounded him. The little sermon of Lulu Day, although delivered in wrath, had its effect upon him. He began to feel how very mean it was to torment any thing merely because it had no power to harm him, and with the feeling dawned the consciousness that Dick Jones was not a good boy. This consciousness was strengthened into firm belief when, on the morning following the sermon, he saw Dick take the turtle that he had sold the day before, and he resolved that he would have nothing more to do with him.

Lulu encountered Albert on her way to school in the afternoon.

The little girl's eyes were red from the tears that had fallen at the misery they had looked upon, and she was walking on, feeling very unhappy, and not noticing the beauty of the day, or the birds that sung with all their power to charm, when Albert said:

"I'm very sorry about the turtle; it was very mean to burn it."

Lulu was startled by the words. She looked up and saw Albert.

"The turtle is dead now; you killed it!" she said.

"Oh! no, it isn't; Dick Jones picked it up this morning close by your gate, and carried it off—it was right lively."

"It's dead, and we're going to bury it this afternoon, Thode and I."

"Where did you find it?"

"Thode took it away from Dick Jones this morning. You see I had tied my mark upon it, and it was there when my brother found it."

"I'm very sorry!"

"So am I."

"May I come and help bury it?"

Albert spoke with such evident sincerity, that Lulu could not refuse his request, and so it was arranged that Albert should be present.

Dick Jones was on his way for the

cows just at the time in the afternoon when Thode, Lulu, and Albert were putting the turtle into the ground.

He called over the fence: " Come, Albert Elder, come on for your cows."

"I'm not going yet; you needn't wait."

"Needn't I? You are civil. I say, what are you doing there?"

Theodore Day called out: "We are finishing your work; you may come in and see."

Without the slightest idea of the meaning his words conveyed, Dick jumped over the fence and joined them. A small hole had been dug in the ground, and the dead turtle was lying beside it.

"Whew! what's the matter now? Is the thing dead?" asked Dick, and he put out his foot to turn it over, but Lulu darted forward in time to prevent his touch upon it.

"You've killed it with matches and pins, and now it's dead you shall not kick it. I wanted you tied up to a tree and pricked; but papa said it was wicked, and that I ought to ask to have you forgiven instead of punished; but I should think you'd be afraid of getting hurt in some way, you're such a bad, wicked boy."

Theodore put the animal in its grave. The sight of Dick made Lulu too indignant to cry just then, and she threw the fresh earth in, whilst Dick walked away without speaking one word.

The turtle's grave was made. Theodore laid the green grass back in its place.

"Will you forgive me?" asked Albert when it was done, and Theodore had gone to put the spade in its place, and no one was near but Lulu.

"It wasn't my turtle that you hurt; it was God's property. He made it, and you must ask Him to forgive you for killing it," said the little girl, as she turned away and went to the house.

Albert Elder felt very uncomfortable. He knew that he was doing wrong day by day, but he did not know the way out of the thicket in which he was entangled. He was wasting his time, that priceless gift, given of God, as the material out of which we are to carve a mighty destiny for good or for evil, and he felt that the evil had possession of him.

Slowly he walked on in the direction of the meadows, where he had driven the cows in the morning. Dick Jones was evidently waiting for him. Albert saw him in the distance, sitting on the top-rail of a fence; but he was in no haste to join him, he would have chosen not to meet him that night, but Dick waited with great patience until Albert came up to the place where he was sitting.

Then Dick jumped down from the fence, and walked on for a distance without speaking.

"I should like to know what you are thinking about, and why you can't just as well speak to me? You are as stiff as if we never had a race on the river together, nor after peaches in Langdon's orchard. Forgotten them days, haven't you?" said Dick, at last.

"I wish I could forget them, and all the mean things I've been engaged in for the last year," replied Albert.

"Getting pious, are you? Then it's time for me to be off. Next time you want any help about carrying freight, you'll call on me, won't you?"

This last allusion was a bitter one to Albert Elder, for it brought painfully to his mind, the first theft in which he had been engaged, and the fact presented itself with it, that if it had not been for Dick he should have been caught and punished, and for his mother's sake, Albert was thankful to Dick.

"Dick Jones," said he, "I mean to stop short stealing and idling and the town. I'm going to work or to school, or any thing to lead a different life, and if you'll join me and work in earnest, we'll be friends; if not, I don't want to talk with you, or have any thing to do with you."

"You've got into better company; you'll be proud as the parson's daughter now. Well, we may as well part; may be we shall anchor in the same harbor in some storm yet, and you'll be glad to remember me," said Dick.

The boy liked Albert Elder in his indifferent way, and was sorry to be left by him. But the thought of trying to change his life was not to be entertained for one moment. The habit of sin was not to be easily thrown aside with him. Nothing less than a moral tornado would sweep away his cloak of wrong-doing, and show how terrible a thing it was.

The two boys parted without another word. Albert to drive his cows to their owners, and Dick to do the same with those under his charge.

Albert was positively unhappy. Dick was angry, and knew not the cause; angry at himself, at Albert Elder, but more than all, at Lulu Day. Her words rang in his ears, and would not hush themselves into silence.

*4

Chapter Three.

ALBERT ELDER had not the slightest idea of his own weakness as he crossed the Housatonic River on his way home, the same night that Lulu Day cried herself to sleep over the sorrows of the dead turtle.

He thought that he had only to leave off spending his time in the street and to devote it to some useful purpose to become a happy boy.

He had not left the bridge when he met his sister Fanny. She was running toward the village as fast as possible. She almost passed Albert without noticing him.

"Where now, Fanny? what is the matter?"

"O Albert! I am so glad to see you. I was going for the doctor—mother is very sick, won't you run?"

Albert forgot the true meaning of her words in his eagerness to be doing something. "To be sure I will, and be back in no time—you run home and say so."

Albert was not long in finding the person whom he sought, and in returning with the doctor.

The house was in confusion, neighbors were hastening to and fro, anxious to do some kindness, but in entire uncertainty as what it was best to do. Fanny was crying, "Do something for mamma, make her speak to me; do make her open her eyes and say one word;" and in the excitement no one thought to comfort her until the doctor said : " Never mind, Fanny, we will bring your mamma back in a few minutes, if you will be very quiet and not disturb her." Not another word uttered Fanny. She waited and waited on in silence until it was long past her bed-time, sitting in a little chair near the bed and watching every movement. She was made happy at least by the doctor, who said: " Now you may come and speak to your mamma."

" Dear mother, I thought you were gone away to leave me for always," said Fanny. " I'm so glad you've come back."

The mother tried to speak to her child, but in vain. Paralysis had laid its deadly hand upon her and made her its prisoner.

"What is the matter with my mother? Why can she not speak to me?" questioned Fanny, and she looked up so pleadingly into Doctor White's face that he took her hand in his and led her out of the room.

"My dear child, your mother can not speak to you now."

"Will she never say any thing again?" sobbed Fanny; and Albert stood by listening eagerly to catch every word.

"We hope so. I think she will be able to talk after a few days, but she knows all that you say and if you cry or say any thing to show

how sadly you feel it will hurt her: can you be a little heroine, and put on a bright face when you go in to see her?"

Fanny's idea of a heroine was rather confused and dim, but she understood perfectly what the doctor meant by a bright face, and she promised at once.

"Here is a good chance to try my new resolution to lead a different life," thought Albert, and he commenced with great zeal, being determined to pass the night in watching his mother. He wanted something to do every moment, for he could not endure to stop and think over the past, and, in action, he thought, was his only happiness.

Fanny fell asleep sitting in her little

chair, and was carried away for the night. One by one the neighbors who had gathered in the excitement of the hour went to their homes. Doctor White left and the house was quiet.

"You had better go to bed, Albert," said the woman who was to remain with Mrs. Elder, when all were gone.

"No, I thank you; mother might get worse and then you would want me."

A grateful look from the eyes of his mother as Albert said that, gave the boy positive pain, and yet he knew not why.

"I can call you," replied the woman.

"But I sleep very hard, it would take you half an hour to awake me; I shall stay up."

This was spoken so positively, that nothing more was said, and Albert picked up a book and tried to read. He had formed no habit of reading; it gave him no pleasure, and he soon dropped it. Then he began to think over the year that had gone. Conscience whispered to him that if he had tried to save his mother from care and trouble as he might have saved her, possibly the illness would not have been.

It seemed to Albert Elder that some one had painted a picture of his life and that it was hanging directly before him, and hiding his mother lying so pale and still on the bed in the same room.

There were the many times when he had run away from school, during the last year; each one rising out of the past and accusing him with its pointing finger of neglected duty, and then the sins that had grown out of the one. They seemed a forest to him, and he saw himself entangled in it. The untruths that he had uttered to shield himself from reproof; the little things that he had taken without thought at the time; how they had grown into huge branching shadows. Albert felt himself overwhelmed by them. He knew not what to do, except to try and do better in the future, but that resolve gave him no comfort.

He could bear the silence—broken only by the ticking of the long cased clock in the corner—no longer. His heart ached heavily; he wanted to breathe the fresh air, and he went out, believing that he should feel better there.

It was a clear, bright night. The moon was nearly down, and the stars shone out of the deep blue of the vault above like immortal eyes.

Albert could not endure their gaze. He sat down under an apple-tree that was white with blossoms, thankful for its shade from the accusing eyes of the stars. The insects were only humming out their happiness into the ears of the night; but to Albert they seemed to scream: "You're a naughty, wicked boy; you've left your poor mother to do all the work, and now she is sick and may be going to die; you're very bad, and you deserve to ⸺erable, and we are glad you

Now the insects, rejoicing in their brief existence, were utterly unconscious of acting as an accusing voice for conscience; but Albert wished them all dead. The poor boy was utterly miserable. He could not bear the silent room within the house, and he could not endure the solemn night out of doors.

Suddenly the thought was suggested to him: "Perhaps, if you were to ask your mother to forgive you, you would feel better."

Acting upon the impulse, Alrbet rushed in, startling the woman who was bending over Mrs. Elder, and striving to catch the words she sought to utter.

"Come here, Albert; it may be you can tell what she tries to say."

Albert bent over his mother. Her lips moved; she sought to articulate; he laid his ear close to her lips, but the sound was not formed; she could not speak.

"Perhaps it is Fanny that she wants; you had better bring Fanny in," said Albert, anxious to devise some means of securing a moment alone with his mother.

No sooner was the room left to them than Albert threw himself on his knees beside the bed, and said: "O mother! I've been such a bad boy to you, won't you forgive me, and I will be kind to you always, just as long as you live! Say you forgive me, or look at me; do, dear mother!"

A quick expression of joy pervaded

the mother's face. She tried to speak to her boy. Words would not come, but one hand was put forth toward nim. It quivered and fell upon the covering. Albert caught it up and guided it to his own head. The fingers tightened a little, a feeble clasp was all the token that they could give, but it was a mother's sign of full forgiveness, and it filled Albert's heart with joy for the time.

Fanny was brought in, only half out of her dreams. She scarcely knew what the scene meant until the rigid face of her mother aroused her.

"Hold me near, let me kiss my mamma," said she; and Albert held her in his arms.

"She don't kiss me, won't she never again," asked Fanny.

Fondly beamed the eyes, for a moment upon the little child, and then they closed in sleep. Fanny was taken back to her rest, but Albert persisted in his determination to remain until morning. He fancied that it would be a kind of expiation for duty neglected in the past. He did not know that one expiation satisfieth for the whole world, and that without faith in that, man's best efforts are in vain. Albert Elder was trying to do **right** in his own strength.

Chapter Four.

WHEN Dick Jones was on his morning journey to the meadow the day following, he would have felt very mean if his consciousness of honor had ever been called forth, for he had been acting on the principle of revenge against his former companion.

A feeble sense of justice made him hide behind a tree when he saw Albert in the distance, but knowing that the cows would betray his being in the vicinity he determined to brave it through, and so he walked boldly on and met him.

Albert's first impulse was to walk by on the further side of the road, but the strength of his determination to avoid all intercourse with him failed, when he thought of his kindness on one occasion, and so he said kindly:

"Good morning, Dick!"

"Humph! The mother's scolding made you amiable, I guess. I'll try it again," was the response.

"Try what again?"

"Just hear yourself talk, Albert Elder! making believe you don't know what I mean."

"I've done making believe any thing, Dick. I do not know what you mean."

"Didn't you catch it last night?"

"What?"

"A scolding."

"From Lulu Day! Yes, and I deserved it."

"From your mother, I mean."

"No, I did not."

"You'll make me believe that in a hurry. You ought to have seen her eyes snap, when I told her about hookin' over to the dépôt."

"O Dick Jones! You did not tell her that, tell me that you did not."

"Of course I did. Did you think I was going to let you slip off and get pious without a word?"

"Dick, Dick, what have you done?"

"It wasn't me that did it. Don' you know you'd got the things all down by the river, and couldn't get a blessed one of 'em into the 'Bonny Blue,' if I hadn't helped you, and the tide was running down like a mill stream too?"

"O Dick! mother is very sick; she can't speak one word to any body. she hasn't said any thing to me since I saw you yesterday."

"I don't believe a word on't," said Dick stoutly, but a sudden fear made his heart quake. He felt as if it had been thundering very heavily, and might again, and as if he was exposed to danger from some source.

"It is very true, and I'm afraid your story helped it," said Albert.

"'Twasn't my story, 'twas your stealin' did it."

Albert felt the truth of the statement too forcibly to contradict it, but a great feeling of rage took possession of his soul. He felt as if he could take Dick Jones up in his arms, and squeeze him to death without the least sorrow. He was angry at Dick, instead of at himself, for being the cause of the story.

"You've killed my mother, you are a murderer!" he shouted forth, as Dick was stealing along the hedge, apparently trying to rinse the dry dust from his bare feet, in the heavy dew that lay on the grass.

Albert stooped down. A stone lay temptingly in his path. He picked it up. Surely he could not be about to hurl it at the boy before him. Once or twice he turned it over. He squeezed it as hard as he could in his hands. Something whispered in his ears, "Where are your good resolutions?" and quick as thought, Albert hurled it with all his might into the river. He heard the splash. So did Dick Jones.

"Hurrah! what is that?" cried Dick, and he parted the hazel bushes and crept through, to see what had caused the splashing in the river.

Albert Elder saw him go, and, lest a second stone should tempt him, he ran away from himself and from Dick, who, when he returned to the highway saw no one. He wondered what had become of Albert; he looked for him in vain, until he reached the long bridge. On its further side he saw the boy hastening home.

A strange desire took possession of Dick, to know if the story that

Albert had told him was true, and without fully forming any intention, he found himself crossing the bridge. Once across, he hastened on. Every thing about the Elder cottage was just the same as when he had crept cautiously up to it the night before, except that Fanny was not tossing apple-blossoms under the tree. The d or was widely open, and the warm sunshine flooded the floor. Dick was led on by an irresistible impulse, on, into the house.

No one met him. It was very still. There were no signs of breakfast in the kitchen. Dick stood still to listen.

The rumbling of wheels came up the road. It was Doctor White's carriage. His obedient horse obeyed the sign, and before Dick could run, (for Dick was afraid of Doctor White,) that good man had entered the house, and laid his hand on Dick's shoulder. Dick jumped half across the room.

"What on earth are you doing here?" asked Doctor White.

"I came to see if Mrs. Elder was sick."

With a tight grasp on the boy's shoulder, lest he should run away, the doctor led him into the room where Mrs. Elder lay. Dick would have escaped but for the iron fingers that held him.

Fanny would not leave her mother's side. She had clung to her ever since the morning began. Albert was looking at her through tears that were rushing down his cheeks, blinding his gaze. He saw his own work before him. If he could only tell her *all*, how good he meant to be every moment of his life, that would be some comfort; but now she did not seem to hear any thing.

"How is this?" asked the doctor, and he led Albert out of the room and shut him out.

"Fanny! Fanny!" said Doctor White.

"Oh! I'm bright, *isn't* my face bright? I washed it ever so much this morning, on purpose." said the little girl, and she gave a woefu' smile that had no joy in it.

"It looks very clean, go and play with your kitten, it is waiting for you on the steps outside, there is a good child."

Fanny obeyed from habit. She would have gone and played with the gate just as soon, if she had been bidden to do it.

Mrs. Elder lay quite unconscious. Doctor White looked troubled as she gave no sign of knowing that he was present. He had forgotten that Dick was in the room, until that boy ventured near the bed.

"What's the matter of her, be she dead?" asked Dick in a whisper.

"You here! you vagabond!" said Doctor White, forgetting for a moment his intention regarding the boy.

"You held me in," whispered Dick. "I didn't want to come a bit."

"Had she any ill news yesterday, that you know of?" questioned Doctor

White of the neighbor who had been in the cottage through the night.

"No, she came into our house yesterday morning, along about eleven o'clock, and she was as bright as ever I see her I didn't know as she had any trouble but her boy there, he used to bother her mind a little, she alluz said 'twould come out right in the end she hoped."

"What happened after that?"

"Nothing that I know about."

"Was any one here in the afternoon?"

"Nobody but this boy, Dick Jones, wuz here, 'cause I see him coming in just after 'twas night."

"What did you come for?" questioned Doctor White.

Dick felt as if he was in the pres-

Far of all the judges in the world, would must answer for his life; so he said: "I came to tell her about Albert."

"What about him?"

"Why, you see we'd been carrying on like something together all winter, and he got good all to once, and wouldn't speak to a feller."

"What did you tell Mrs. Elder about her son—out with it, quick!"

"I told her 'twas him as stole the bundles out o' the depôt, over to Derby, awhile ago, and put 'em in the Bonny Blue."

"You little vagabond!" almost cried the doctor, and his iron fingers closed around the boy's arm, as he hurried him out of the room.

Dick finished his story under the

apple-tree. The doctor heard him patiently to the end, and then pointed out to him the gate, and bade him go out of it.

Albert had heard every word of Dick's story, and it pierced him sorely. Whatever he might do in the future, he felt that the past he could never remedy, and he hid away from the physician's eyes, feeling that he could not bear their look of accusation.

Poor Alfred! He was trying to hide away from himself, and knew not the refuge to which he might go.

Doctor White was too angry to trust himself to say any thing to Dick Jones, and reserved his lecture for a future opportunity. He gave the needed advice for the morning, comforted Fanny by words of promise, and the wheels of his carriage rolled over the stones, and down the hill, to the village over the river.

Chapter Five.

TO Dick Jones's darkened mind it was a great mystery, how Doctor White could think his story had hurt Mrs. Elder. It is true that the physician had not put this thought into words, but Dick felt that it was so. And as he heard the rolling of the carriage following him, and even the sound of the horse on the bridge, he certainly made all possible speed across it, and darted behind the nearest object that could hide his ragged person from the eyes that had once looked upon him that morning.

Dick was bent on mischief. He felt a wicked pleasure in having made Albert Elder suffer, even if it was through his mother; and having achieved one point, he at once began to prepare for a trial in another quarter, and that in the direction of Lulu Day.

To that end he passed carefully along the river-bank in search of another turtle, but turtles was either forwarned or preöccupied, for not one was in sight, and the boy was forced to give up the battle in that direction. Suddenly he remembered that he had had no breakfast, and a feeling of hunger sent him in the direction of his home.

Now this home of the Jones family was not unworthy of notice. It had been for many years the home of a family, that by one of the mysterious ways of Providence had gone down lower and lower in the scale of fortune and of popular opinion, until it had actually gone out in the town of Derby.

There were dark whispers that the grandfather had sailed dark ships over the seas, and returned laden with the spoils of a pirate; that his gold had melted away like ice under a burning sun; that God had written annihilation to that family for their ill-gotten gains.

The house itself was separated from the village. It had once been a comfortable residence, but now, alas! dilapidation had hung its airy banners out of the windows, and the chim neys carried aloft the same dingy flag. For a long time the roof had sheltered no tenant. People shook their heads gravely when it was suggested that the Rock House might be occupied, as if the shadow of the sin yet rested upon the dwelling, where the sinners had used their ill-gotten riches.

At last, when a new mill came into being and new workmen came into the town, one was found to live in the Rock House. How it ever came by its name none knew. It was located in a small valley just outside of the village and yet not far from it.

It was gravely whispered that the shadow of the pirate had fallen on the Jones family; but the better informed portion of the community knew full well why the stern hand of poverty held it in so close a grasp.

Every spot of earth in New-England is lovely in the time of the fruit blossoming. The pink and white snow scattered over the trees, and the flakes fluttering down to the ground every moment, fill one's heart with gentle promises of the future, when the snow shall have melted into more delicious substance. Even Dick Jones felt this as he drew near his home in need of his breakfast. He dashed his hand against a bough full freighted with blossoms, exclaiming: " Hurry now, old-pear tree, and grow your pears; I wish I had one this minute."

"They won't grow none if you knock the poseys all off; mother says they won't," exclaimed a little girl, coming out from the shelter of a lilac bush.

"Halloa, Dolly! Have you saved any breakfast for me?"

"Yes, *most all of it;* mother said 'you'd be so hungry' that she wouldn't give me but a little tiny bit."

"That's just because you want some more, Dolly."

"No it an't," said the little girl, with a corner of her apron very near the place where tears grow, and a little sob in her voice, "for I know you won't give me none, you never do, you wouldn't if I didn't get a crumb."

"Well you don't drive cows, and

chop wood. Get out of my way, Dolly; I'm in a hurry."

"I get hungry, just as well as you do, Dick," said Dolly with a sour look on her round lips as she followed Dick within doors.

"It seems as if you could get home sooner if you tried; it isn't so far that you have to go," said Mrs. Jones, as soon as Dick entered with an imperious demand for his breakfast.

"May be *you'd* better go and drive the cows yourself," was Dick's wicked reply.

"Dick Jones! I *won't* have you for my brother not another single bit of a minute if I can help it, 'cause you talk so to my mother, and she hasn't had a bit to eat to-day, 'cause she wanted to save it for you. You're a bad wicked boy, and you'll go to the bad place when you die and get all buried up, I know you will."

"There! take that for your sermon, Dolly Jones," and with the words a blow fell upon Dolly's bare arm. She was half frightened and half hurt, and ran to her mother who had paid little attention to the words of her children.

At the instant the sound of the blow reached Mrs. Jones's ears, she was taking Dick's breakfast from the stove.

"Mother! he struck me! Dick Jones struck me just as hard as he ever could on my arm," said Dolly, who really believed that some terrible injury had been inflicted upon her, and for a moment the room resound‧ed with her cries.

"It is good enough for her, she may let a fellow alone!" exclaimed Dick, in reply to a glance from his mother's eyes.

"I didn't hurt him. I—never—struck — him — not — once," sobbed Dolly, holding fast her arm to cover the bruise she believed to be there.

"Dick! Dick!" moaned Mrs. Jones. "did ever a mother have such children? It does seem to me that you can't be together two blessed minutes without getting into a quarrel."

"I want my breakfast," growled Dick, "I'm nearly starved."

The patient mother made haste to put it on the table and stood by, watching the boy, until he had consumed the last morsel. Before the meal was ended, Dolly had sufficiently recovered to take her station behind Dick's chair in the hope that her brother would give her one taste of his breakfast; but no, the last crumb disappeared, but not into Dolly's waiting mouth. Dick pushed back his chair without noticing the look of disappointment that shadowed Dolly's face which was still tear-stained; or that his mother looked more careworn than usual.

"Dick," said Mrs. Jones, "will you split some of those large sticks in the yard so that I can burn them to-day?"

"I should think you'd go out and set the woods on fire. I don't see what you want to burn so much wood for. I split enough yesterday to last a week," answered Dick.

"She used the last stick to keep your breakfast warm," said Dolly, who imagined that she was always to stand on guard to defend her mother.

"I don't believe it," ejaculated Dick.

"Very well then; you will please to bring me in an armful," quietly said Mrs. Jones.

Dick went into the wood-yard. Not a small stick was visible. Now Dick knew perfectly well that dinner could not be cooked without wood; but he played around for a few minutes, putting a few of the large logs that had been sawed, into position for splitting; then he went for the axe, carried it out to the pile, laid it down, and a moment later Dick's feet were disappearing over the ridge of land that concealed the village.

As no strokes from the axe reached the house, Mrs. Jones looked out. Of course, Dick was not there.

"What shall I do?" groaned Mrs. Jones. "That boy has run off, I am afraid."

Dolly rushed out of the house. In a moment she rushed in again exclaiming: "He's gone, I see just the top of his head jumpin' up and down over the hill."

Mrs. Jones sat down for a moment in real distress. She knew that her husband would be at home for his dinner, and it seemed beyond her strength to drive the axe into one of round logs that lay outside, and she had little hope of seeing Dick again until hunger should drive him home.

Dolly Jones had inherited her mother's nature in very large degree, but the circumstances of her young life had turned it into a harder channel, so that stout resistance had taken the place of gentle deference to all but her mother.

Dolly was not a pretty child. She was very plain. Her face was freckled and her hair was red. She had auburn eyes, that were about two shades deeper in color than the fur of the red squirrel. Dolly never had had a new dress, not since her baby-days. She would have been almost frightened at the sight of one, and if such a thing had been possible, she would have expected to see Dick catch it up and declare that he was going to carry it off and have a jacket made of it; for poor Dolly was so accustomed to being set aside for Dick in every thing, that an idea of any thing as her very own had never been entertained for a moment by her. Whatever Dolly's faults were, and she had many, she had one sign of a true heart. She loved her mother, and she always wanted to stand up and fight for her whenever she thought her to be abused.

This occasion was one of Dolly's opportunities. As her mother sat down in despair, Dolly looked at her old and ragged dress, wondering—"If any body would see it if she ran very fast, as fast as ever she could, after Dick to bring him home."

"I should think something dreadfully awful would happen to Dick, he's so ugly to you," said Dolly.

The thought was dismal comfort to the boy's much-loving mother, and she said in a very low voice: "Don't, Dolly, you don't know what you are talking about."

"Yes I do, mother, it's about Dick. I think it would be just right if he got punished. You never whip him, and father don't, only once in a big long while, when he gets awfully mad at him. Let me run and catch him."

Mrs. Jones said nothing. She was thinking of a row of little graves away in a distant State, without a sign to tell to any eye but her own, that they were the graves of her children. For the moment the small mounds were before her. There were six of them. All taken away from her in three years. The pretty infant; the once tottering child, that just had learned to lisp a word or two—dearer to the mother's heart than all the languages on earth; and the manly little boy, whose life was growing into promise, day by day. Every one of the six passed in review before her, and the mother groaned in agony.

The sound of her own lamentations aroused her. She looked around for Dolly. Dolly and her sun-bonnet (in her hand instead of on her head, for she had not had the time to put it on) were half way to the village.

It was just at the hour when the street was traversed by many little feet on their way to school. But the feet of the school children were carefully covered from the summer's dust, and Dolly's were deep in it. In the haste of the moment, the little girl had rushed on, and she found herself in the midst of neatness and good clothes before she was aware of it.

A sense of her unfitness came into her mind. The freckles on her face deepened suddenly, and the auburn light in her eyes burned brightly, as a boy called out from the opposite walk. "There goes Dolly Jones! I say, Dolly Jones, are you taking that sun-bonnet down for a pattern, to get an iron one cast by it?"

Dolly put on the offending sun-bonnet. The sides fell down over her face, but she was glad of that, she wanted to be hidden from sight.

Some one touched Dolly's arm. She flashed her eyes around from under an angle of the hanging bonnet, half expecting to see the rude boy at her side; but no, it was a little girl.

"I wouldn't mind, if I were you, what that boy said, it was very unkind of him, but then he don't know any better," said the little stranger.

Dolly stood still, and her little comforter stood still, and the two children looked at each other for a very few seconds.

The comforter was very pleasant to look at. She made Dolly think of the pretty blossoms on the apple-trees, that were so pure and bright. And then her dress was marvellous in Dolly's auburn eyes, for it was just "the very color of the posies on the peach trees, up in the orchard," she thought.

There were the gentle, brown loving eyes of this little girl looking right into the anger-kindled fire of Dolly's.

Dolly was the first to speak. "I ran down in a great hurry, 'cause mother wanted Dick," she said, feeling that some excuse was demanded by the picture of neatness before her, for her own shabby appearance.

" What Dick ?"

" My brother Dick—Dick Jones."

" I'm sorry you have such a wicked boy for your brother."

" So am I, with considerable emphasis, said Dolly. " Do you know how naughty he is? He ran off just now, 'cause mother wanted somebody to cut some wood for her, and she hasn't any, not a bit of a stick to get dinner with."

"I'm very sorry. If I see him on my way—I'm just going to school—I'll tell him; and I'm sorry the boy over the way was so unkind to you."

"Never mind him. What's your name?"

"Louisa Day, but every one calls me Lulu, and so may you."

"I shan't ever see you again," said Dolly, with a mournful little accent, that breathed of a world of tenderness underneath the freckles, way down deep in her heart.

"Why not?"

"'Cause I don't come down here very often. I shouldn't now, only Dick ran off."

"Where do you live?"

"The folks call it the Pirate's house, but my father isn't the pirate."

"Oh! I know, down in the pretty little dell. I should like to live there; I think it's nice."

"There an't any glass hardly in the windows, and it's all holes," said Dolly.

"Oh! but I should want it all fixed up, and made nice if I lived there."

"I'd rather have some shoes to wear, and a purty dress like yourn."

"May be you will have, some day," said the little comforter.

"I never had a new dress in my life."

"O dear!" said Lulu Day, and she knew no word to fight away the sad fact, but her eyes filled with tears as she looked at Dolly, and thought how very plain she was, and ragged too. "I must go on now, or I shall be late," she quickly added, "but I'm going to take a walk to-night, and I'll come and see where you live, if you'll let me."

"Oh! do!" said Dolly, delighted to think she should have the pleasure to think of all day. She had nearly forgotten Dick when Lulu passed on, and I do not know when she would have remembered her errand again, if Dick's head had not suddenly appeared over a fence as she was passing by.

"A pretty-looking show you've made of your rags, Dolly Jones, right here on the street. I should think you'd be glad to keep out of sight."

"Dick! Dick won't you come home now? Mother wants that wood *so* bad!" urged Dolly, as her brother's head disappeared as suddenly as it had come into sight. The fence was too high for the child to look over, and there was no opening that her eyes could penetrate. She called again, but no answer came. Dick had caught a glimpse of Albert Elder, who was walking that way, and not wishing to be seen by that boy, he had made his escape through a garden, and thence along the river bank.

After a few minutes Dolly started on her way homeward, being quite certain that Dick was not to be seen any more by her in that vicinity. Ere long she heard footsteps, and looked to see who was approaching.

"O Albert! Albert Elder! you

don't know what a naughty boy our Dick is. I wouldn't play with him another bit if I was you," said Dolly, who had waited until Albert came up.

"I don't think I shall," said Albert quite solemnly.

"I'm real glad of it, just to punish him. He's gone off and hid, and won't come home and cut some wood. What's the matter with you?" Dolly's auburn eyes were not bestowed upon her in vain; they told her that Albert Elder was in trouble.

"My mother is very sick, I'm afraid she is going to die," said Albert.

"O dear!" said Dolly. "Why don't the doctor fix her?"

"The doctor can't make her talk,

she can't speak a word," said Albert, with a kind feeling toward Dolly for her sympathy.

"Has she lost her tongue?"

"She can't move it, only a little bit. She can't do any thing more than a baby can—but I must hurry. I'm carryin' these things home, so's Miss Miles can make her something good." And Albert went on his way across the long bridge, leaving Dolly to find the Rock House.

"O mother! I saw him, peeping over Mr. Stearns's high fence, and he wouldn't come home, he's gone off somewhere," called Dolly, as she went in at the open door. There came no reply. "Mother! mother! where are you?" shouted Dolly. Still no answer, and Dolly listened. The house was deserted. The little girl was tired, and the day was getting warm, but minding neither her tired feet nor the sun, she ran out into the yard. Mrs. Jones was not in sight.

"I wonder if mother has gone into the woods to pick up sticks," thought Dolly; "yes, I do believe she has, 'cause the basket is gone. I'll go and see if I can't find her."

Dolly sped away up the hill and down by the river. The winter's breaking up brought down from the wooded region above much drift-wood, that became entangled in the low growth along the shore. This drift-wood was considered common property for any one who had enterprise enough to gather it; but it was no easy matter, first to work one's way down through hemlocks, brambles, rocks, and shrubs to the river's edge, and then to get possession of the dried bits and carry them back, fighting the way at every step.

Dolly had little doubt but that she should find her mother somewhere on the bank. Her kind little heart began to reproach itself even for the few, pleasant moments spent in talking with Lulu Day. Perhaps if she had hastened home her mother would have let her go for the wood, and Dolly began to think that her mother must be very hungry, having eaten no breakfast; for the pain of hunger was already oppressing her, and to stop it for the moment, Dolly filled her mouth with the bright green leaves of the wintergreen that grew at the feet of the laurel in her way. The little girl plunged into the thicket. She scratched her bare feet with the briers of the blackberry, and the hemlock branches did not seem to mind, in the least, slapping her in the face every moment. It was quite dark down by the river, and all at once a feeling of loneliness came upon Dolly. "Mother! mother! are you down there?" she shouted, glad to hear the sound of her own voice.

Some crows that were busy robbing a cornfield at a distance answered her with a miserable answer of Caw! caw!

"Mother! mother! don't you hear me?" cried Dolly, pushing her way a little deeper into the thicket where

the answer of the crows came less
distinctly to her ears. Dolly's feet
began to bleed from the many briers
that had been thrust into them,
to smart with the pain.

"O dear! I must get out of this.
I don't believe mother is down here,"
said the child, and she strove valiantly
against branch after branch that stood
guard over the way, sometimes catching her feet in the gnarled roots of
old trees, and sometimes getting a
severe stroke from a rough bough that
crossed her way. Dolly was exceedingly tired when she reached the highway. She looked up and down, but
no soul was in sight. For a moment
she was undecided whether to search
further or go home. "Mother must
go past here on her way back, and,

I'll wait and help carry the basket," thought Dolly, and she went under the shade of some old pine trees and sat down to rest and to wait. There was not one blade of grass under the trees, neither was there room for one, for the ground was covered with dry, yellow needles from the pine trees overhead.

Dolly played with them, gathering many together and then scattering them again, until tired of that, she lay down and looked up at the great branches over her head and wondered how they ever grew so high and so wide, and if they liked to have the wind move them about so, and if they ever felt afraid in the dark and stormy nights. Then she began to wonder what it was that made her afraid down in the shadows where the river ran and roared so, and why she couldn't have a dress just like the peach posies, and pretty brown eyes, and go to school as Lulu Day did, and why her mother didn't come, so that she could tell her about the visit that was to be that day. Dolly thought of all these things, and then she looked up again into the branches and thought of the God that her mother had told her about who lived in heaven and made the sun; and thinking, in her childish way, of Him, sleep came and touched her eyelids, and slowly, slowly the fringe fell lower and lower, shutting out the whispering pines, shutting out all wonder of any thing on the earth, until not a vestige of her auburn eyes could be

seen. A few birds looked in at her under the shadowy covert, and doubtless thinking that she was comfortable, they twittered a little and hopped away, leaving her to her rest. Kindly nature guarded the little sleeping child until the sun had reached the meridian. A farmer was on his way to the region beyond, and chanced to look down by the river-side and note a little bundle of clothes lying there.

He spoke a word or two to the steady veteran of a horse, and the horse stood still. "I think I'll see what that is—it isn't just the place for a scarecrow," thought the farmer, and he, half vexed at the feeling that would not permit him to go by and leave it, scrambled down to the place where Dolly lay.

"I declare if it isn't that little girl that lives down at the Rock House," said the man to himself, as he looked into Dolly's sleeping face. Dolly did not move.

"Here! here, child! Wake up! this isn't the place for you to be sleeping in," said farmer Stone, and he shook Dolly gently. She started at the touch and sprang up only half awake.

"I—I—was waiting for my mother," she said, trying her utmost to call back perfect consciousness.

"Your mother; why, it's dinner time and my wife will be waiting for me; don't you ever go to sleep in the woods again and make an old man like me get out of his wagon to see what's the matter," he said, as he started to regain the highway.

"I'm sorry. I won't do so again," said Dolly, following him. Mr. Stone spoke a second time to his veteran horse, and it started on its way to to the Stone farm, leaving Dolly by the road-side. That little person watched the horse and wagon out of sight, and then, fully awake, she started for her home.

"Why, Dolly, where have you been all the morning, I've been so worried about you!" exclaimed Mrs. Jones the minute Dolly appeared.

"Why, mother, I came home and called and called you, and I thought you'd gone into the woods to get sticks to burn, and I went to look for you, and I couldn't find you nowheres at all, and I sat down to wait for you to go by, and I went fast asleep until a man came by and woke me right up. Mother, where did you get that wood? how nice it is cut!"

"I must have been up-stairs when you called me. I did go into the garret to see if I could find an old box or barrel that I could cut up. Poor child! how tired you look!"

"I'm hungry, mother; but did Dick come home?"

"No, he did not; but who do you think appeared to cut the wood for me?"

"Father?"

"No, Albert Elder. He said you told him Dick wouldn't come. I heard the axe, and I looked out and saw him at work."

"It was real kind of him," said Dolly.

Mr. Jones appeared, ate his dinner in silence, and went away. Dolly never talked much when he was in the house, for she was afraid of him.

"Now I wonder where Dick can be," said Dolly, as the sound of the workmen came down to them from the distance. The dinner-table had disappeared long before Dick's return.

Albert Elder was trying his very best to do right. He thought he was forgiving Dick Jones when he went to cut the wood for his mother; and no sooner was that done, than he hastened back, anxious to be present should there be any thing for him to do; but the day passed on without much change.

Chapter Six.

LULU DAY was faithful to her promise regarding the visit to Rock House. She felt an interest in the little girl who had never had a new dress, much as she disliked her wicked brother, and Lulu secretly resolved that Dolly should have a nicer dress than any she had ever yet worn; but Lulu kept this resolve a secret. Her visit was ended, and she was on her return home, when she met Dick Jones with a string of fish fastened to a stick. He carried them over his shoulder; but no sooner did he catch a glimpse of Lulu's pink dress, than the fish were thrown on the grass, and one, larger than the rest, was singled out, and detached from the string.

Now, it so happened, that there was no house in sight, at the point where Lulu met him, and she felt a little afraid to pass by, but she did not for an instant think of running.

"How do ye do, Miss Day, and how's the turtle since the funeral?" called Dick, just the moment he came within hearing distance.

Lulu did not answer; she kept straight on, as though she had not heard him.

"Now, Miss Day, won't you take a fish instead of the turtle? It's nice and fresh, and you can carry it just as well as not."

Lulu's first impulse was to tell him to go on his way—she knew he did not intend that she should take the fish; but she suddenly resolved that since he had offered it in the stead of the turtle, that she would accept it, and also carry it home; it would seem more like having forgiven him if she did, and Lulu desired with all her heart to forgive the boy.

"Thank you!" she said, "but how am I to carry it?"

Now, Dick had not the slightest idea that Lulu intended to take it, and so he said with the greatest seeming interest: "Oh! you wait one moment and I will fix it for you. I dare say you never touched a fish."

"I never did," replied Lulu

"This is pretty slippery you'd drop it in a minute, if you tried to carry it in your hand," and Dick, with a malicious smile, went about to put a bit of a branch through the gills, and then he offered it to Lulu.

She put out her small hand to take it, clasping it firmly, and said "Thank you, you are very kind to give this to me."

"Well now, I never see the beat o' that. In all my life; I wouldn't a believed the parson's girl had so much spirit in her. She can preach pretty well, but I do believe she acts better'n she preaches." thought Dick, as he stood and watched the pink dress, until its owner was out of sight. Now Dick expected every moment to see Lulu Day stop and throw the fish down; but no, she carried it home, and Dick in his heart, if the boy had a heart, began to admire Lulu Day.

Any boy but Dick Jones would have hesitated about going home, after having run away under the circumstances that he had; but he went boldly in, threw down his string of fish, and said: "Here, mother, are some fish; I caught 'em down the river to-day, and I want some for supper too."

"Why did you go away without cutting me the wood this morning?"

Dick gave a loud whistle for answer, and strayed out of doors.

"I wouldn't cook *one*, if I was

you, mother; I just think he ought to go to bed without any supper."

"And so do I, Dolly."

"Then, why don't you make him?" questioned the child, her auburn eyes flashing out a brilliant light.

The answer of Mrs. Jones was not given, for a strange face stood within the doorway. Something in its glance spoke of evil tidings.

Mrs. Jones went forward to speak with the man.

"I'm sorry, ma'am, indeed I am," said the man, "I wouldn't have come if it could be helped, indeed ma'am, and I wouldn't."

"What is the matter?" asked Mrs. Jones, her face turning pale and paler every instant. A faint gleam of the truth flashed upon her as she saw a wagon slowly wending its way down the hill from the village.

"It's your husband, ma'am; they're bringing him home."

"Is he dead?" calmly asked Mrs. Jones, and Dick's horror-stricken face echoed her question.

"O dear! no, ma'am, he's alive, but it's pretty bad, he's pretty much mangled up. You see, he went round before they could stop the works."

"O dear!" gasped Mrs. Jones, and she would have fallen before the stroke, but for the great necessity for exertion on her part.

But a few minutes passed and the wagon with its sad freight was at the door. It so happened that Doctor White was passing the mill at the time of the accident, and he accompanied the hurt man to his home.

There was a great bustle about getting him out, and getting him in, and then the wounds had all to be dressed, and two broken bones to be put into place, and the house was in confusion until it was quite dark, and then it was left to its occupants. Dolly was very quiet and very helpful. She was horrified by the accident that had befallen her father. It was the first time that she had ever felt sorry for him, it was the first time that she had loved him. But a ten-fold deeper feeling for her mother took possession of her heart, and it was beautiful to see the childish tenderness with which she sought to give her aid; and all the while Dolly was wondering if God had made her father hurt, and if it would make him any kinder to her mother.

'Well, now, it is curious how troubles come into a town in company," said one neighbor to another, when the Rock House was deserted for the night.

"They always do," said another. "I never knew it to fail: there's the widow Elder struck down with paralysis; and Mrs. Brown's child you know fell into the river; and Peter Carder's mother-in-law fell down stairs and broke her arm; and now, here's Paul Jones most killed in the machinery. I do wonder what'll come next — something, you may be sure."

"I declare! I've forgotten all about my cows till this minute," exclaimed Dick Jones, "but I guess somebody's been after 'em afore this time," and as it then was quite dark, all thought of going for them was abandoned.

Just as Dick had spoken, a low knock on the door called Dolly to open it.

"Don't be afraid, it's only me," said Albert Elder. "How's your father? I'm very sorry to hear that he is hurt."

"Won't you come in? He's better since the doctor took care of him," said Dolly. Dick darted out of sight behind a door that chanced to be ajar, the instant he heard the sound of Albert's voice.

"No, I thank you. I only came to

tell Dick that I brought up his cows to-night, and will drive them back again in the morning if he isn't able to go. I heard what had happened, and thought he wouldn't think of them."

"Thank you, Albert, you're real good to be so kind, and about the wood too; I'll tell Dick."

"No! no! Dolly, I am *not* good,' murmured Albert even after the door was closed, and he on his way to the gate.

Albert Elder was very miserable. All day he had been performing acts of kindness, but they had given him no real pleasure, not even when he was driving the cows for Dick, who had so meanly betrayed his evil actions to his mother. From this, doing kindness to his greatest enemy, he had expected to find comfort, but he did not. He saw before him that pale fixed face of his mother, and a finger pointed at him whichever way he went, and a voice sounded in his ears, and the finger wrote, and the voice said: "Look! it is your work."

Albert tried to think of other things, to whistle and feel happy, but every moment he was only getting more and more wretched. It seemed to him that there wasn't any thing real in life but sickness, and hurts, and death, and after that ——! Albert did not want to think of what came after that to the wicked, but it was all the time in his mind. He came to the long bridge over the Housatonic, and he sat down on a stone on the Birmingham side of the river, and put his young face on his hands, and thought. All the years of his past life seemed to be like a long picture unrolling before him, and they all seemed so vain, so good for nothing, that the boy began to moan, not loudly, not as loud as the pines, but only a piteous accompaniment to the flow of the river; and Albert wanted to pray, but he did not know how. All the prayers of all the men that he had ever heard seemed to him then as idle words; he did not want the things that they had prayed for, but he did want an angel to come and comfort him.

All at once Albert threw himself on his knees, with his arms across the stone, and his face on his arms. "O dear! what shall I do?" he sobbed. "I don't want to live, and I don't want to die."

The river must have held its peace and the wind hushed itself to rest for an instant, to carry these words to a human being who was near.

Rev. Mark Day had heard of the affliction that had befallen Mrs. Elder, and had been to see her.

On his return he was tempted to stop when across the bridge, and look at the river with the western moonlight falling upon it. He was comparing the stately progress of nature through her yearly round with man's ever-changing destiny, when the words of Albert Elder were borne to him. He was at first startled. Could it be some one down by the water's edge contemplating suicide, and had Providence sent him there to arrest the deed?

In haste to help a fallen mortal, Mr. Day hurried down.

Albert heard the crackling of the undergrowth beneath the minister's feet, and he was frightened. What could a man want, hurrying down the bank so at that time in the evening—was he going to drown himself! Albert kept very still to see what he would do, but a ray of moonlight revealed the boy to Mr. Day, but revealed him only as a boy; his name he did not know. Mr. Day did not know Albert Elder's face, not even when the boy had risen and the moon shone full into it.

"What is the matter, my boy? I

thought some one was in distress; I was positive that I heard some one say: 'I don't want to live, and I don't want to die.'"

Albert felt at that minute as if he should like to be down close to the river's edge, where he could, at least, dive under and be for a moment out of sight and hearing. He began to feel ashamed of his distress, as if it had all been foolish, and he said: "I believe I'm a big baby sometimes; it's nothing."

"How do you know that it is nothing? I am certain that it was true distress that made you utter the words that I heard. Come! sit down on this rock and tell me all about it."

Now Albert had been longing all the day for some one to whom he could go with his story, and, besides, the boy was tired with all the work that he had done during the day, and he longed to open his weary heart at once; but something held him back. I think it must have been the spirit of evil who did it. Albert did not answer.

"Come, my little friend, I used to have a great many sorrows when I was a youth of your age, and I always felt as if I wanted some one to whom I could tell them all. I am sure that you must feel as I did, do you not?"

"Oh! yes, sir!" said Albert.

"Well then, it's a very nice place down here, and I want to help you; won't you let me?"

"I'm afraid you can't," said Albert.

"Oh! I'm so wicked, and you can't make me any better, sir."

"No, I can not, but I know who can."

Albert had seated himself on the very stone across which he had thrown his pleading arms only a few minutes before, and wished that God would send an angel to comfort him.

Now the angel that he had wished for was come, but Albert wist not of it.

He hid his face in his hands, but there was no need of hiding it, for nature had done that by shadows. He said: "Mr. Day, you don't know what a bad boy I have been; I've been very unkind to my mother when she was so good to me, and I'm afraid

I've killed her;" and having given the burden of his grief, the boy's head dropped lower yet, and the tears fell where the dew could not penetrate, on the dry leaves by the rock.

"Who is your mother?"

"I thought you knew me," replied Albert, "my mother is Mrs. Elder."

"I have just been to see her, and was on my way home when I heard you."

"And will she ever get well?" was the question that was asked almost before Albert had time to give it a thought.

"Never well, but better I trust."

"I've been so wicked to her for a whole year. I haven't hardly once done what she asked me to, and now she can't speak to me to ask me to do any thing; if she *only* could, it seems to me that I'd work always to please her."

"To please whom?"

"My mother, sir!"

"And isn't there some One that we should strive to please more than father or mother?"

"I suppose you mean God, but He is so far away."

"Don't you think that it is He who makes you feel that you are wicked, and that sent me here to find you to-night?"

"Sent you here!" exclaimed Albert, and the boy trembled with terror at the thought.

"Certainly, I believe that our Father in heaven, who numbers the very hairs of our heads, governs every circumstance of our lives. I believe that He has sent me here to comfort you; and now will you tell me all your grief?"

Very kindly the minister listened to Albert's story of his special sins, even to the theft that Dick Jones had participated in, and then Albert ended with the story of the turtle, telling all the part that he had enacted in that affair.

"And you wish to leave all this wrong behind you and lead a different life, I hope," said Mr. Day when Albert had ended.

"Oh! yes, sir! and you don't know how hard I've been trying all day, and that's what makes me so unhappy; I don't feel one bit better than if I hadn't tried. I thought I should be happy if I was only good."

"And have you been good all day?"

"I've done all I could!" replied Albert, with a heavy bit of despair in his voice that failed not to reach Mr. Day's heart, and touch it with tenderness for the boy.

"Now, my friend, let me tell you a story," said the kind man.

"I knew a little boy once who was very much like you. He knew that he had been doing wrong all his life. Something kept whispering in his ears: 'What would become of you, if you should die to-night, if you should fall down and break your neck, or if the lightning should strike you, or if you were to get drowned?' This boy was very miserable, and he thought he would leave off all his bad habits. He would play with wicked boys no more, and he would do every thing his father and mother bade him to do, and he thought then that he should feel happy. It happened that the more he tried to do well, the more temptation overcame him, for the boys that he deserted because they were evil, were angry, and did all in their power to persecute him for the desertion. This only made him worse, for he wanted to revenge his own wrongs. This boy that I am telling you of, went on in this way for many weeks. He did not give up trying. Every morning when he got up he would say to himself: 'Now *to-day*, I will not answer back, I'll bite my tongue off, before I will let wicked words fly out of my mouth; I will not let my face wrinkle up once when I'm told to do any thing that I don't want to; and I'll be very kind to Benny and Harry.' But when night came, he would have to confess to himself in the silence of his own heart, that not one of his resolutions had been kept, and conscience would write out a long list of sins that he had committed that day.

"At last, the sins had grown into such a long array that the boy was frightened. He did not know what in the world he could do with them. They fell on him like a mountain weight, and between the fear of death on the one hand, and the mountain weight of sins on the other, the little fellow came near being crushed; but some one came in and helped him."

"Who was it?" almost gasped Albert Elder, who felt just as if he *knew* that little boy—as if the minister had been telling him *just what was in his own heart.*

"It was Jesus Christ, our God's dear Son."

"How could He help him?"

"I will tell you how He did help him. One night this boy was terribly frightened, so much so, that he could not bear the agony another minute. There was a terrific storm, and he thought he should be killed before morning, and he went down in the night to his father, and told him how wretched he was, and how he had been trying so many days to do right, but couldn't: and his father told him the story of Jesus; how it required the Son of God to die to take away the sins that he was trying to hide himself; that his child was trying to do the work of the Redeemer."

"And was he?" interrupted Albert.

"Yes, he was trying to forgive his own sins and hide them away back somewhere in the past, out of sight, when Christ had promised to hide them all with Him in the mystery of His death—to hide them so securely that they would not rise up against him in the judgment."

"I *wish* He'd hide mine," said Albert, "I would be so glad then."

"Have you asked Him?"

"I didn't know how, and I'm afraid."

"Would you be afraid to ask your mother to forgive you?"

"No, sir, she loves me very much."

"And that is the reason why you should ask God, because He loves you so much. This is true that I have been telling you. This boy went to His Father in heaven, and told Him all the story, just as you have been telling me yours to-night, and begged God to forgive his sins, because Christ died to save him, and to help him to do right. Well, would you believe what a change this prayer made in that boy? His mountain weight of sin, that had been growing larger and larger every day for many days and all his life long, suddenly vanished away, and his fear of death seemed to have buried itself in the mountain. Whenever he thought of the future world, it was that Jesus Christ would be there to save him, and to welcome him. This world grew more beautiful. It seemed nearer heaven, and it had so many things for his hands to do to help others to do right, that he thought if he should live never so long, he could not tire of telling the story of what Christ had done for him."

" And was it easy to do right after that?"

" Yes, because you know he had Christ to help him. When he was tempted he whispered, 'Dear Jesus, won't you help me?' and Jesus always helped him, when he asked it so; but oftentimes the boy did wrong, very wrong, and then he was wretched until he got back into Christ's heart by prayer and sorrow for his sins."

"What became of the boy?"

"He grew up to be a man."

"And was he always happy?"

"No, not always, *because he did not trust Christ*, his Friend and his Saviour, as he should have done. He let the world get in between, and sometimes his feet got torn, and his heart was weary getting back all the long distance that he had wandered; but when he did get there, he *always* found Christ *waiting* for him, with loving welcome."

"Where is he now? I should like to find this man, and tell him how I feel, for I know he'd feel sorry for me; I don't want to live and I don't want to die," murmured poor Albert.

"That boy is the man who is sitting by you now, and he does feel sorry for you."

"O Mr. Day! *you* are a minister, and you *preach* in the church. Were you ever such a naughty boy as I am?"

"I was; and I want you to ask God to forgive you for Christ's sake, and help you to do right."

"Perhaps He'll hear you, when He wouldn't me," said Albert; "won't you please to ask Him to do it?"

"I will ask Him for you, but you must ask Him yourself. He hears every child that cries from the earth toward heaven."

"I do hope He will hear me, I shall die if He don't," thought Albert, as the kind minister knelt down on the dried leaves in the thicket, and prayed to the kind Father of souls to have mercy upon the boy, to forgive him for the past, and to show him the pathway leading to heaven.

Mr. Day prayed for the very things that Albert felt that he wanted, that he *must* have, and all the while his hand was laid on the boy's head, that rested on the rock beside him; and when he besought God to have compassion on the mother who lay ill, and to restore her to her children, Albert sobbed out his petition with all his heart.

A certain feeling of safety came into Albert's soul from the prayer of Mr. Day. He felt comforted by it.

"I thank you, but I can't tell you how much," he said, "for finding me down here; I wanted so much to tell some one how I felt."

"Well, now you will know whom to tell. God is always near you. You know that whatever happens no one can separate you from Him, and His ear is always open to every word you may speak. Go to Him and tell Him all your wants, and all your hopes, and all your love."

"Will that be praying?" asked Albert, as Mr. Day arose to leave the leafy covert that had been their closet of prayer.

"Yes, that is prayer. We tell our

joys and sorrows because we want sympathy; we beg for favors because we need them. No one can sympathize with, or pity us, or bless us perfectly, but God. You must trust Him for He will make you happy."

Mr. Day and Albert had reached the bridge where they must separate.

"Good-night, my friend," said Mr. Day. "You must come and see me and tell me every thing. We must friends after this."

"Oh! thank you, sir! you are very kind to me," said Albert. And the two parted.

Albert crossed the bridge hastily. He thought suddenly that he had been long away from his mother, and he might have been needed at home.

The stars were clear and kindly in their light upon the boy. They did not strike him with their burning rays as they had done the night before, as he walked on, but beamed gently out of the beautiful vault above, and Albert felt for the first time in his life that the stars were his friends beckoning him in the right way.

As he drew near home, sounds from voices met his ears, and he knew that some new event had taken place in his absence. Aunt Hannah Elder had arrived. Having heard of the illness of her sister-in-law, she had made all possible haste to starch her caps and put her apparel in order for a short absence from home, and her arrival occurred at the same time that Albert was telling his troubles to Rev. Mark Day on the river-bank.

Now, in the light that we poor, blind human beings cast upon events in this world, this visit of Aunt Hannah's was the most unfortunate event that could have come to Albert Elder. He disliked her more than any one that he knew, for she had spoiled many a day's happiness for him when he was a very little boy at his grandfather's house, and he never could get through one day with her in comfort. How, then, were the new resolves to prosper under the perpetual irritation that Aunt Hannah was certain to occasion?

Albert's heart sank within him, as he opened the door and saw her sitting in his mother's rocking-chair, and urging it to and fro with great velocity and determination. She made it squeak awfully but she didn't mind that, not in the least, but the instant Albert's fingers pressed the door-latch she lifted her finger in warning.

"It's that boy!" she exclaimed.

Fanny had been very much awed by the presence of her aunt, and subdued to a degree of silence that was unusual to her. She wondered what boy her aunt could mean.

Albert went in.

"Take care there! Don't make one breath of noise, your mother is very sick!" said Aunt Hannah, in a whisper that penetrated to every corner of the two rooms.

"Is she worse?" asked Albert, in a low voice, and he went directly past his aunt, as if to go into the room adjoining where his mother lay; but the wise woman had no idea of any such proceeding, and she seized Albert by the arm; rising to do so, the chair she had occupied flew back, hitting the door and making more noise than Albert and Fanny combined would have done in half a day.

"How do you do, Aunt Hannah?" said Albert; "but I must go in and look at mother!"

"*No, you must not*, the doctor has been here, and he says she must be kept quiet."

"Did he say Fanny and I were not to go in?"

"No, he didn't say no such thing. He knew I'd have more sense than to let you."

"But mother likes to see us, I know she does, and she tried last night to speak to me; I must go in, Aunt Hannah, and you mustn't try to keep me away."

A sound as of a voice trying to escape into the air came from the inner room, and Albert shook off the grasp on his arm and darted in.

"Well! well! if boys will be so wicked, what am I to do? I wish I had the training of that one, one week, I'd see!"

"Albert has been real good, since mother's been sick!" said Fanny.

"Is that what you call goodness?" Sharply as Aunt Hannah turned around upon poor, little, frightened Fanny, the child had the courage to say: "I don't think it's very bad for

Albert to want to see mother. He never went to bed last night, and he sat in the chair right by her bed, most all the time, and it didn't make her no worse."

"A boy like him sitting up all night! Who ever heard of such folly?" muttered Aunt Hannah, and she drew near the door of the room into which Albert had gone so unceremoniously. "If he an't a talking to her!" thought Aunt Hannah, and she was about to stop by force, if necessary, such a proceeding, when Albert met her.

"Aunt Hannah!" he said, "nobody can keep me away from my mother She knows what I say now, and I *must* speak to her. I want you to go out, and Fanny too, and let me shut the door for just a few minutes, and then I promise not to talk to her again to-night."

Albert spoke with all the strength of his nature, and for once Aunt Hannah obeyed the request without the slightest resistance. The door was closed, and Albert threw himself on his knees beside his mother's bed, and told her all the story: of his disobedience, and his sins; of his misery, and his sorrow; of his efforts to do better, and their failure; of his meeting with Mr. Day, and his prayer for him; "and, mother, I'm going to try with all my heart to love God, and be a good boy," he said, when he had finished his story. In telling it, he had clasped one of her hands in his; from time to time the feeble pressure that it gave assured Albert that his mother understood what he was saying, and when at the end he told her of his intention to do right, her lips moved, and with a mighty effort they formed the words: "God bless you!"

Albert heard them far down in his heart, and it throbbed violently as he asked: "And, mother, will you forgive me for being disobedient to you so many times?"

The pressure of her fingers, and the sweet look of assurance that beamed in her eyes, told Albert the glad tidings that his heart longed to hear, and kissing her fondly many times, Albert whispered "Good-night!" and went away.

Aunt Hannah did not speak to him

when he asked her what he should do for her.

"I'm dreadfully sleepy, Albert, and I'm afraid to go up-stairs in that big room, all alone. Won't you go with me?" asked little Fanny, who never had slept away from her mother before.

Instead of an irritable reply that Fanny really expected, Albert went with her.

"Albert, what's the matter with you?" Fanny asked, as soon as they were beyond the hearing power of Aunt Hannah.

"The matter? Nothing's the matter now, but there has been this long time; I've been a very wicked boy."

"An't you going to be no more?"

"I hope not."

"Will you be good to me?"

"I will try. Come and say your prayers."

"Why, Albert! *Will you hear me?* You never did."

"I will now."

"Mamma let's me pray just what I've a mind to, will you?"

"Yes."

Fanny kneeled down beside a chair in the full moonlight, and Albert kneeled also.

"Now, Albert, put your arm around me, just like mother does, or I can't say 'em. There, that's right; now you are sure you won't feel bad 'cause I ask God for something?"

Albert assured her that he would not, and Fanny began her prayer with "Now I lay me down to sleep."

When that was ended, she prayed: "Dear Father up in heaven, my aunt Hannah has come here to day, because my mother is sick. I don't love her one bit. She's cross, and she don't love me a bit more'n I love her. Won't you please to make mother get up off of the bed again, so's she can go back to grandfather's house, where the little children are all growed up so's she can't strike 'em? Please, God, bless my mother and my brother, and make him a good boy, so's he won't run off any more, and leave mother to cry when Dick Jones comes and tells what a bad boy he's been. Don't let him pull my hair any more. Amen."

"There! you see I had to pray just what was in my heart to pray, and you mustn't be cross at me," said Fanny, rising up and standing just in the window-frame of moonlight, that lay across the carpet. Albert caught the little white figure in his arms, kissed it with a love in his heart that never had been there before, and then he tossed it as high as he could, and it fell right into the midst of the best feather-bed in the guest-chamber. Just as he did so, a little noise was heard down the stairway.

Aunt Hannah had deemed it her duty to look after Fanny, and to see that she was properly committed to the angel of sleep for the night. To that end she had, in her carpet slippers, softly ascended the stair-case, just in time to hear Fanny's prayer.

Every word of it had gone home to her heart, as she stood at the door and saw the two kneeling figures, and she felt the entire truth of Fanny's statement: "She don't love me a bit more'n I love her." When Albert lifted Fanny in his arms to put her into the high bed, Aunt Hannah crept down the stairs as noiselessly as possible, and she seated herself in the rocking-chair again, and thought of her own past life, and of the days when she had been a little girl. Thinking of those days brought her nearer to Fanny and Albert, and awakened a feeling of sympathy for them, that if it could only be made to live and grow, would blossom into love and tenderness, but it all died away as

Albert overturned a chair in the room above. He had been waiting till Fanny should fall asleep, and in crossing the room he had hit the chair. The noise that it made, broke with a sudden snap the feeling of sympathy in Aunt Hannah's heart, and when Albert had groped his way down the dark staircase, he met with no welcome salutation from that lady; but he was not in a mood to mind her cross words, he went about to make the necessary preparations for the night, and then asked her if she was to take care of his mother.

"What else have I come for? That *is* a pretty question for you to ask; I should like to know who else there is in the house, or in the family for that matter, to do it *but* me. They've all got family cares enough of their own, if I'm any judge."

"Well then, Aunt Hannah, I'll say good-night. If I can help you any, you must call me; I'll try to wake up."

Albert received his aunt's stately "good-night!" and went to bed, but not to sleep. His whole soul felt alive, and burdened with a prayer. He watched the moon go down with a feeling very unlike that of the previous night.

Albert had never known before what it was to pray, but he knew then, when his very heart seemed to go up to heaven with the prayer for his mother's recovery. The thought came to him that God knew best what was for her happiness, and that he would do whatever was best for them all, and comforted by the thought he fell asleep.

Chapter Seven.

"PAPA! Papa! exclaimed Lulu Day, the very instant that she heard her father's footstep in the hall, "there's been a man here to see you, that wanted you in a hurry. He said Dick Jones's father had got very much hurt, got all caught in the wheels and carried round and round before they could get him out, and he was afraid he was going to die, and wanted to see you; and mamma went with the man, and told me to tell you, just as soon as you came home."

"I will go at once; what are you doing, child?"

"Nothing, only waiting for mamma to come home."

"Can you get ready in a minute to go with me?"

"Yes indeed, papa, in half a minute," and Lulu sprang into the hall, hat and sacque in hand. She was ready to go without them, as Dolly Jones had been in the morning of the same day, but her father insisted that they must be put on before she started.

It was quite an event in Lulu Day's life. An evening walk with her father, was an indulgence never before granted, and she entered upon it with great pleasure.

"It's a long walk, papa. I've been

there to-day, and there's a little girl lives there, Dick's sister, and she isn't the least like Dick; I quite like her. You see, a naughty boy made fun of her across the street this morning, and I took her part, for I was sorry for her, and so to-night when I went to take a walk, I went to see her. She's very, very—well, she isn't pretty, papa."

"Lulu, are you not sorry for this terrible accident that has happened to Dick's father?"

"Certainly, papa! What made you ask me such a question?"

"Do you remember wishing that something might happen to Dick?"

"Oh! oh! dear me!" exclaimed Lulu, at once lost in the horror of the thought.

"You don't mean, papa, that my wishing for something to happen to Dick had any thing to do with this awful accident?"

"Perhaps not, but I only wished to show you how blind we are in our wishes and our revenge. You wanted something to happen, and so I have brought you with me, that you may see what it is to have something happen."

Lulu would have withdrawn her hand from her father's, and gone home, if she could have done just as she had chosen.

It was a cruel visit to Lulu, one that her father would willingly have spared her, but he knew that she would never forget the lesson that night learned.

The wounded man was in great agony. He believed that his final hour on earth was fast drawing near, and for the world to come he had made no preparation. Now pain held him in its thorny fingers, that clasped him tighter and yet tighter every minute. In the intervals of acute suffering he would cry out for some one to pray for him.

His wife had prayed for him all the days of her married life, prayed for him silent prayers, unknown to any one on the earth. But she was a weak woman to resist any thing that was stronger than herself, and she had never tried to deter him from any course upon which he had entered. She never resisted any thing, not even poverty and rags, as most mothers would have done. She loved Dick, as mothers will love the child that causes them the most trouble, and to Dolly it seemed that the worse he grew the more she tried to do for him, but put her prayers into words she could not. When Mr. Day and Lulu reached the old house it was all astir.

Dick was swinging on the gate, glad to get rid of all the trouble inside, and wishing to run away somewhere, and not come back until the fuss was all over.

"How is your father?" questioned Mr. Day, as he stopped before the gate.

"He's going on like any thing," answered Dick, in no hurry to get down and let them enter.

"Why don't you stay with him?" asked Lulu.

"If that an't Miss Day! I declare I didn't expect to see you again to-day. Pray how's the fish?"

The boy did not seem to have the smallest portion of an idea of deference, or reverence for any thing or any body, but he left the gate as he spoke.

"You're a wicked boy to talk about fish at such a time," said Lulu, hesitating an instant to speak to him, as her father went in.

"Fish is a deal pleasanter than what's inside," said Dick, but curiosity led him to follow Lulu within.

The strong hope for life that Dr. White had given, was based upon the wounded man's keeping perfect ly quiet, but quiet he would not be, not for an instant. "I shall be still enough for all that you can see in a short time, but where shall I be *then*, what will become of me? Do you think a man that's going into eternity without any thing on earth to travel with, is going to be quiet just afore he sets out? I tell you I won't be. Where's that minister?"

"I am here; can I do any thing for you?" said Mr. Day's calm, assuring voice, for he had entered the room, leading Lulu by the hand, just in time to hear the question.

"O my child!" exclaimed Mrs. Day, rising up, with her eyes half blinded by tears. "This is no scene for you," and she would have led Lulu forth into the pure air outside, but a hurried whisper from her husband stayed her hand.

"Mamma, I wanted to come with papa," said Lulu.

Dick stood up in a corner, as far from his father as possible, and affectionate little Dolly had her head in her mother's lap, covered up with her mother's apron. Of all the frightful things that she had ever seen, her poor father was the most frightful; and her mother had told her that nothing more could be done for him.

"You are the minister, and your business is to tell how to be saved. I am going to die, and I want to know, quick!" and the man tried to raise himself in his eagerness, but fell back. For a moment he suffered too much to listen to any thing.

Mr. Day kneeled upon the floor, close beside the bed of Mr. Jones, and besought him to repent and pray for forgiveness, while yet there was time.

"I don't know how! You might just as well tell a child to read, before he knew the letters," exclaimed Mr. Jones.

Still kneeling there, Mr. Day told the sweet story of God the Father's love; and Christ the Saviour's sacrifice for sin; and the very house itself seemed to listen, it was so still.

"I've never done any thing for God never minded a word about Sunday, or any of them things," groaned Mr. Jones.

"It isn't your good deeds, nor mine, nor those of any man that we come to plead; it is Christ's good deed. Do you think God will find any fault with that?"

"I wish I'd thought of these things before; I'm in torture now."

"Then come to Christ, and He will give you peace and rest," said Mr Day.

"Peace and rest! peace and rest!" murmured the poor man, as if they might be dreamed of, but never experienced in this world.

Lulu went and whispered softly to Dolly, "I'm very sorry for you," and not a word of comfort did she attempt to give.

Children must have comfort of some kind, and Dolly held Lulu's hand fast in hers, whilst Mr. Day prayed to the merciful Father, to look down in kindness and pity on the afflicted mortal who lay near to death. He besought, most earnestly, pardon for the soul that had strayed so far from righteousness, and that, for Christ's sake, it might be accepted into the family of the redeemed.

The room was very still during the time of Mr. Day's prayer. Dick had never heard any one pray who seemed thoroughly in earnest before; and Dick could not tell how it happened, nor can I, but at the conclusion of the prayer, he found himself on his knees in the corner of the room. He got up hastily, and glanced around, to see if any one had noticed him feeling half ashamed of his late position—ashamed to have been seen kneeling before the Maker of heaven and earth! Was any human feeling so utterly absurd as that?

Dick's mother had watched him, and taken note of every action.

All the words of comfort that could be spoken, were kindly and truthfully given. And then Mr. and Mrs. Day, with Lulu, went home. What a contrast it was! with its home-neatness everywhere visible, and even coming out to meet them through the clearly lighted windows—to the dim and dismal house that they had just left.

There was yet another prayer sent up that night to heaven; and the petition bore on its wings the boy who had gone down in his sorrow to the bank of the river, and the strong man stricken in the midst of health, and not ready to go hence.

Chapter Eight.

THE following morning Mr. Day called again at the Rock House.

Mr. Jones was too weak to talk, and Mr. Day did not see him; but he talked cheerfully and kindly to Mrs. Jones, assuring her that, out of the present cloud, blessings would surely arise.

By the light of day, the place wore a forlorn aspect, and Mr. Day reported the condition of the household to his wife. That lady went to the Rock House laden with articles of comfort Theodore and Lulu were her delighted aids in the enterprise.

It was a very difficult thing to do, to arouse Mrs. Jones to the effort of putting her own house in order, when it never had been in order since the time of her going into it; but it was so skilfully and kindly done, that the woman was not even made aware that she was reproved for want of neatness.

"How has your husband been during the night?" asked Mrs. Day, as soon as she went in.

"Very poorly, ma'am, till 'most morning, and then he got a little quiet."

"He's quiet now?"

"Oh! yes, this hour and more, he's scarcely moved."

"Then, do not you think that we might make the room look a little pleasanter, before it will be time for the doctor to come?"

Mrs. Jones looked around, despair visible on her face.

"I don't know as I can do much to make it look better, it's a poor old shell of a house any way."

"Oh! I think we can. Let us try, But first, have you had any breakfast?"

"Yes!" said Mrs. Jones, but the word was very faintly spoken, as if the breakfast had not been very strength-giving.

"We've had some bread and gruel," spoke up Dick, who had entered just in time to hear the question regarding breakfast.

"You ought to be ashamed," whispered Dolly, close to his ear, as she passed by.

Dick made a motion with his hand, very much as if he would strike her, but suddenly looking at Theodore Day, it dropped harmlessly by his side. Dolly was safe from that blow.

"Dick!" said Mrs. Day, in the pleasantest voice in the world, or so it seemed to him, "don't you think that you can find me some wood, something that will burn up nicely and quickly? Thody, here, will help you, for I wish to make something for your father."

There was magic in the voice and the manner, and Dick did not resist. Never in the history of his wood-getting, had he been known to move with such alacrity. In a very short time the kitchen fire blazed brightly, and the kitchen was perfumed with savory odors

Now, not Mr. Jones alone was the

consumer of the "something nice to eat," that the minister's wife prepared. Dick appreciated it fully, and Dolly began to wonder if folks that wore pink dresses, and looked so pretty and clean, could cook, and wash dishes like other people.

The hot water, with the aid of soap and a good stout house-cloth, did wonders in the way of brightening up the dingy place. Mrs. Jones was quite ready to work, if only some guiding spirit would tell her what to do.

For the first time in many days, the floor was clean around the store. The chairs were dusted and put into orderly array. Even Dick was won over to the wonderful employment.

Mrs. Day took out from her stores

a snowy cover for the table beside Mr. Jones's bed, and it made even the dingy, cracked cups, that stood upon it, look better and brighter.

Dolly could scarcely keep within bounds her curiosity, as she watched the minister's wife on her round of duty.

A new era was dawning for Dolly Jones. The poor, homely bud was to have kinder showers to blossom in than nature had bestowed on her slow growth.

"There comes the good doctor! You're just in time," said Mrs. Day, as the worthy man appeared in his gig on the summit of the hill, that lay between the Rock House and Birmingham.

"There's that old pail left right

there!" cried Dolly, whose eyes had espied a pail in an unseemly place, and she attempted to carry it away.

Poor Dolly! her foot caught in an uneven board, and down she went upon the floor into the midst of the flood from the pail, just at the instant that the door opened to admit Doctor White.

Dick laughed, and cried out: "Now, Dolly Jones, you're prettier than ever."

Theodore Day sprang forward to lift up Dolly, with a glance that Dick described afterwards as fastening down on him like a rainbow.

In a minute the doors between the rooms was closed, and Dolly's mishap shut away from curious eyes.

Theodore Day helped Dolly from the floor. Her dress was dripping from the water; her face was very red with mortification, and with anger at Dick for his unbrotherly remark. She looked very much as if she would like to drop down somewhere out of sight, and Dolly thought instinctively of a large empty barrel in the cellar, just under her feet, as being a very haven of refuge for her, but then she stood for a moment in her uncomfortable plight not knowing what to do

"Come up-stairs with me and get some dry clothes on," said Lulu, half laughing at the odd dismay of Dolly; but unwilling that that little girl should see her face, she stooped down and picked up the pail, that had rolled until it could roll no further. It had stopped against the high sil. of the door.

"Come, Dolly," said Lulu, and she moved toward the door.

Dolly moved after her, leaving a pathway on the floor to mark her progress, whilst Dick shouted with laughter at every step she took.

The two little girls disappeared, and the door was closed behind them, shutting out Theodore Day, with his handsome, fine face, full of good feeling toward Dolly, and Dick, with his malicious, wicked expression.

Dolly dropped down on a step at the first landing, and looked up at Lulu, who stood just above her, looking as fresh and fair as the flowers and the sunlight.

"Come, you must hurry, you'll get

cold in wet clothes; mother always tells me so," said Luln.

"O dear! What shall I do?" said Dolly.

"Do! Don't sit there, we'll be back in no time. Come!" and Lulu reached down her hand as if to help.

Dolly's hair seemed to grow darker suddenly, and her face crimsoned, then she burst into tears, exclaiming: "I haven't any dry clothes to put on."

Now Lulu had never dreamed of any thing so unheard of, as not having clothing in abundance for any emergency, and she could not believe Dolly's statement.

"Come! Come up into the room where you sleep, and we'll see what we can find."

Dolly did not exactly believe that

Lulu was a fairy, for Dolly had never heard of fairies, but she followed Lulu with a vague faith that something would be found.

"O dear!" cried Lulu, as her eyes fell upon the place which bore the name of sleeping-room.

Dolly thought that she had hurt herself, and drying her tears she asked: "What's the matter?"

"You don't sleep here, do you?"

"Yes."

"Aren't you afraid?"

"What of?"

"I don't know; it seems just like out of doors. These great rough beams, and those little ones pointing 'way up into the roof, and then that stone chimney. I should think you'd be afraid 'twould fall down on you, or the stones would rattle out in the night."

"This house never was finished."

"I don't believe it ever will be."

"Nor I, it's most to pieces. I wonder if little girls used to sleep up here, when 'twas a new house."

"I hope there was more than one, I shouldn't like to sleep up here all alone. I would keep saying my prayers over and over till I got fast asleep. Now let us find some dry clothes."

"I haven't any," said Dolly, very conclusively. Lulu would not be convinced, until she had searched the premises, and found only rags, and clothing that long ago had been cast aside.

A cloud covered Lulu's face at the result of her search, and then the sun came out from the mental cloud, and beamed so brightly on it, that it shone as she said: "You must wait a little while till I come back," and Lulu's feet ran down the wide carpetless stairway into the kitchen.

"Dick Jones," said Lulu, "why don't you take the house-cloth and wipe up that water? Your mother is busy, and you can do it just as well as not."

"What have you done with our duck, up stairs?" asked Dick, not moving in the least.

"Dick Jones, I know what will be done with you, if you don't behave better to Dolly and every body else."

"What, pray?"

"You'll go to prison, and may be get hung!"

Lulu was sorry for the words, as soon as they were uttered, for she remembered the lesson of Dick's father.

"No, Dick!" she said, going quite close to him, and laying her hand on his ragged jacket-sleeve, "I don't mean that; I hope you will be good and kind to every body, so that God will love you."

Dick's eyes dropped upon the floor, and the evil feeling faded out from his heart. It was the first time that the thought of the possibility of God's loving him had ever penetrated his mind.

Lulu knocked gently at the door of the room where the doctor was dressing the wounds of Mr. Jones, and her mother held a little consultation with her in whispers, and then Lulu whispered to Theodore, and the two went away.

When Lulu reached home her face was very red with the hurry of her walk. Sugar street never seemed so long before, but she did not stop a minute to rest.

Ere long, she committed to Theodore's strong arms a bundle that he declared " bigger than a washer-woman's," and with it he walked back to the Rock House, Lulu following him, and carrying her full share of the burden.

Up the stairs into Dolly's airy bed-chamber, Lulu panted, carrying the bundle that Theodore had borne.

Dolly was sitting by the window, wrapped up in a bed-quilt, for she had taken off her wet dress, and the child was thinking in her vague way that her mother might, perhaps, some day be like Mrs. Day; but how the change could occur, never entered her mind.

"Here! see what I have brought you!" cried Lulu, and she untied the bundle, and out rolled its contents on the floor. An entire suit of her own clothes lay before Dolly's astonished vision.

"Now, see if you did not make something by that unlucky fall of yours; for I shouldn't have known but you had ever so many clothes up here, if I hadn't come and seen with my very own eyes."

Dolly threw aside the bed-quilt, and sat down on the floor beside the wealth of treasure that had suddenly fallen down at her feet.

"I'm *most* glad father got hurt!" she exclaimed.

"O Dolly! If you say that, I shall carry these old clothes of mine right back home."

"Please don't, I didn't mean it, only I never had pretty clothes before. I am very sorry father is hurt, real sorry; if it would make him well any more, I wouldn't put one of 'em on; I'd wear the old clothes just as long as they'd stick on me," said Dolly, and whilst her tongue had been busy, her hands had handled every article.

"I'm real glad that you did not mean it," said Lulu. "You must hurry, for I want you to be all dressed up before Doctor White goes away, and I heard him now, I'm afraid he's going." But Doctor White did not go until Dolly Jones was attired as she never had been before, in the short period of her mortal life. Lulu Day superintended the dressing, as carefully as if Dolly had been a queen, and Dolly was certainly as happy as any queen, for a few brief moments.

Dick had complied with Lulu's request concerning the water on the floor, and then, being very curious to know all that was occuring in the room where his father lay, he went in. No sooner was he fairly within than Doctor White demanded his services in such a manner and with such authority, that Dick was afraid to disobey. He compelled him to hold the bandages and help him in the disposition of them, so that the boy was made to witness the suffering of his father. It formed a deep impression, even upon his hard heart, and once or twice a ragged jacket-sleeve found its way very near Dick's face, and the doctor demanded of him why he was not holding on, with a firmer hand!

At last, it was all over; the wounds were dressed, and the doctor was mounted in his gig to go on his way. At the same instant, Dolly pushed open the door leading from the stairway into the kitchen. Mrs. Jones had just entered the room.

She lifted up both hands in astonishment at the vision of a well-clothed child, and could scarcely realize that it was in very truth, her own.

Dick shouted: "Where's a pail of water? I want to fall down immediately"—and Lulu's face shone with joy, as she slipped past Dolly and gained her mother's side.

"She would look almost pretty if her hair was combed, wouldn't she?" she whispered. "I got the very clothes you told me to; don't you know you put them all together when Mary died?"

"Dolly certainly looks more comfortable," said Mrs. Day to Mrs. Jones.

"I've never had much to fix her up with," said Mrs. Jones.

"A little child is always sweet if only clean and neat, and don't you think any one can be neat wherever they are?" kindly asked Mrs. Day.

"Perhaps so, it always seemed to me that I should keep the house looking better if I had nice things to put in it, and the children too, if their father thought it best to buy clothes for them; but he doesn't very often."

"Let me tell you what I think. I believe that there is not in the world a place but would be endurable to live in, if it were only kept in order; I mean not for show, but for simple, daily comfort, it makes every one happier and it is a Christian duty."

"I never thought about that," said Mrs. Jones, "not as a Christian duty."

During this conversation Lulu and

Dolly were at play under the pear tree that was casting away the last of its leaves of snow.

Mr. Day soon appeared, to visit Mr. Jones. He found him too much exhausted from the pain that he had received at the doctor's hands to talk, but he committed him anew to God who careth for us all, in gentle, pleading tones that went straight to the hearts of those who heard him.

Chapter Nine.

AS Mr. and Mrs. Day walked up the hill, followed by Theodore and Lulu, Mrs. Jones stood in her doorway and wept, and the tears dropped upon the stone step at her feet.

"What's the matter, mother?" asked Dolly, who had gone noiselessly into her father's room to see what he would say to her in her new attire; but finding that he took no notice, she went to find her mother, and saw the tears on the stepping-stone.

"What is the matter, dear mother?

Do you feel bad because I've got these new clothes on and nobody gave any to you?"

"No, my child, I am very glad that you have them, and I'm sure the little girl was as happy as you."

"Then what are you crying for?"

Mrs. Jones found it very hard to find in her heart an answer suited to the little being who looked up lovingly into her face, but the look was so earnest in its love that she said:

"I don't know, Dolly, what is a going to become of us; your father can't work for a long time, even if he lives, and we don't belong to the town to take care of."

"The town?" questioned Dolly,

"what is that, the churches and the houses?"

"No, the people; they pay a certain sum every year to take care of poor people with."

"Mother!" exclaimed Dolly, "you don't mean that you want to go to the 'Poor-House,' to live!" and Dolly's auburn eyes looked stirred to their very depths. "Why, mother! just think what horrid folks live there."

"Perhaps, Dolly, the poor-house here is not like the one in D——; but, I have no idea of going to any 'poor-house' to live."

"I am so glad!" and Dolly sighed to relieve her heart of the burden of the thought, and Mrs. Jones turned away from the door, and went to minister to her husband; whilst Dolly edged her way close under the windows that she might not be seen, and gained the back-yard to tell Dick her story.

Now Dolly had not, in the brief space of her life on the earth, grown so much in any year as she had within the time since Lulu Day touched her shoulder on the street, and comforted her for the words of rudeness that had been given. She had never before been taken notice of by any one that touched her heart and mind. Life was something better and brighter to Dolly Jones since that morning. Dick was leaning against the long well-sweep and looking idly up at the great white clouds that were tented in the sky. Dick was not thinking of the clouds, he was trying to invent something to do that would drive away certain thoughts which had come into his mind through the gates of prayer and suffering that had been held open to his view. Dick was in the uncomfortable state of having ideas that he did not know what to do with, or how to invest, and so Dick was doing his best to contrive a way in which to lose them.

"Dick! what be you doing?" said a voice at Dick's elbow.

"I declare! I wish you wouldn't start a fellow so!"

"I didn't make no noise, Dick, I spoke a'most in a whisper."

"Well, what's the matter?" and Dick moved from the well-sweep to the well-curb and leaned over it. Looking down into the well he watched the drops dripping from the moss on the stones and troubling the dark circle of water.

"Hullo! there's one o' them trouts danced up just then. I'm goin' to draw him up, just to see how he looks; where's my hook?"

"Dick! Dick!" said Dolly, catching at her brother's elbow to detain him. "Don't—don't do that. You know father said he'd whip you awfully if you touched the trout in the well."

"I'd like to see him do it; just you mind your own business, and keep your tongue busy with your own affairs, you mind that now!" and Dick twitched his arm out of his sister's grasp, and in a minute was in the house searching for his fish-hook and line.

Now Dolly knew perfectly well where he had it last and where it was at the time. She waited until Dick was fairly within the house, and then she ran around the corner past the high, old pear-tree, through the garden, and down by the lilac-bushes to a low-lying bit of ground where once had been a stream of water. Dick's hook and line lay on a stone. Dolly caught it up, and tossed it as far as she could into the high grass, and was back again before Dick had completed his search.

"Who's been a fishing with my line?" demanded Dick, out of patience at not finding it.

Dolly was leaning against the wellweep, very near where Dick had left her, when he came from the house.

"Nobody, Dick."

"How do you know?"

"Because, I've just hid it."

"Where?"

"Where you can't find it."

"What business is it of yours? Get it for me, quick."

"Dick! You can't have it."

"I tell you I will!" and Dick's voice arose with his temper; and he went toward Dolly with a very threatening look.

Dolly did not move in the least, except to clasp her arm a little more tightly around the friendly well-sweep.

"No, Dick. Father is sick and he can't punish you; he told you not to touch the trout, and I don't mean you shall; I'll do all I can to keep it from you. If father should die, and be all buried up in the ground, I guess you'd be sorry you touched the fish when he told you not to."

Dick's face turned scarlet with the blood that rushed up to tell that Dolly's words had power in them. For a moment there was a struggle between good and evil in the boy's nature, for Dolly had touched the thoughts that Dick was trying to lose.

"Get the fish-line for me, or I'll strike you," cried Dick, advancing toward Dolly and raising his hand.

"You must strike me then, for I won't get it, if you kill me," said

Dolly, putting her lips together very closely for fear she should scream, for Dick looked as if he wouldn't mind killing some one just then.

"Wait till I count ten and then if you don't start I'll put you down the well," said Dick, and he began to count.

"I shan't get it," said Dolly; "I shan't get it, 'cause I don't want you to do what's wicked."

"We'll soon see who'll be glad to get it. I'll begin once more. Now mind, you start in time."

Dick slowly counted until he reached ten. Dolly did not stir, except that her auburn eyes shook with fear, as they were fixed on Dick's face; for, of all earthly things, she dreaded a well the most.

The instant Dick's voice struck the note of ten, he darted forward and seized Dolly's arm.

"Come, now! I gave you fair warning," he cried. "I told you I'd put you down, if you didn't tell me."

"O Dick!" screamed Dolly, but the scream was a very little one, and Dolly held fast to the well-sweep Dick dragged Dolly's arm from its protection, and in a half-minute she was close beside the low curb of the well. He stooped down and lifted her up, but she held him fast by the neck. Just as Dolly was about to scream for her mother, in mortal fear, some one caught Dick by the collar, and dragged him backward to the ground. Dolly was released in time to avoid his fall.

Before Dick could have counted two, he was lying on mother earth, in a confused state of mind.

"How dare you, you big, cowardly boy ؟ How *dare* you frighten a little girl in that way, and your sister too? I've a great mind to tie you fast to the well-sweep, and dip you in a few times."

"Oh! don't, please don't," said Dolly.

"Well! for your sake I won't; but he deserves it, it would do him good. Dick Jones, if you don't mind your ways soon, you never will. Look here, boy! I'm aching to shake you; and, mind you, if I *ever* do lay hands on you, it will be with a purpose. Get up! Up with you now; and here, take this prescription down to the apothecary's, and be back with it, as if your supper depended on it. No loitering."

Dick got up from the ground, half dizzied by his fall, and wholly confounded by the turn affairs had taken. He turned upon Doctor White a face that would have puzzled any reader of human countenances, and asked: "How did you get here?"

"Get here! If I didn't care any more for that man in there, than his only son does, I should let him die, I suppose."

"Oh! don't, *don't let father die; if you do, we shall have to go and live in some poor-house*," said Dolly, and nervous from her late alarm, she began to cry.

Doctor White had a tender place in

his heart for Dolly, and indeed for all little girls, and he comforted her by the words: "I mean to cure your father, so that he will be better than ever he was in his life."

"What! and bring home his money for mother to buy us things with?" exclaimed Dolly, with eyes widely open, and fixed on his face, as if he were a wonder.

"We will see about that some other time," said Doctor White, kindly patting Dolly's red hair, and thinking in his heart, as he did so, of a little girl that had gone from his home, and that he should one day look for in the heavenly city.

"My brother Dick is a very bad boy; he was going to put me in the well," said Dolly, " if you hadn't catched him just then."

" What for, pray ?"

" 'Cause I hid his fish-hook."

" *That* wasn't right, Dolly. I declare there's trout in this well," exclaimed the doctor, who had been looking down at its moss-covered sides.

" Dick wanted to get the fish out, and I wouldn't let him !" said Dolly triumphantly, feeling quite certain that the right was on her side, and that Doctor White would commend her.

" Whose fish are they ?"

" Father's fish, and he told Dick that he mustn't touch one of 'em."

" And to keep him from doing it, you hid his fish-hook and line, Dolly ?"

" Yes, sir."

"Now, that was naughty in you."

"Why?" and Dolly hung her head, and her freckles deepened.

"Because the hook and line were not your property, and it was not obeying the golden rule. You know what that is, don't you, Dolly?"

"No, sir."

"It is doing unto others just exactly as we should like to have them do to us, if we were in their places."

"I don't know what you mean."

"I mean just this, that if the hook and line had been Dolly Jones's hook and line, that she would not like to have had Dick Jones hide it, not even if to keep her from using it wrongly. Do you think she would?"

"No, sir. But I didn't think about it. Shall I go and find it?"

"Yes, and just as soon as you see Dick's head rising up above the hill, you start and run, and carry it to Dick, and tell him you were naughty to hide it, that that wasn't doing as you'd be done by."

"Shall I tell him you told me to?" asked Dolly, reäppearing from around the corner, just as Doctor White was entering the house.

"Yes, tell him any thing that you like."

Dolly's sentiments concerning Doctor White were liable to sudden changes. One minute she was afraid of him; another she was angry at him, because he made her father groan so, and now she began to think him nearly equal to Mr. Day.

Dolly thought she could find the

hook without the slightest trouble, for she knew just where she threw it; but the grass was high, and the ground was marshy, in remembrance of a stream that once had made its bed there; and soon the little girl was in the midst of it.

The red hair and the auburn eyes were half hidden in the long grass, and so were the boots, the nice boots that had been given to her that very morning.

In her eagerness, Dolly did not notice that her boots were covered with black mud, until she chanced to go in a little deeper than she yet had been. Then she looked down. Dismay filled her heart, as her eyes fell upon her pretty boots, and she forgot all about the hook and line in her new trouble, and turned to seek the nearest way to dry land. She had not gone far when she felt something about her feet. Her first thought was, "It is a snake," and she started to run, but the faster she ran, the more it impeded her progress. It nearly tripped her more than once, before she got safe to dry land. Then she ventured to examine her enemy, and found that it was Dick's fish-line. It had became loosened by being thrown, and entangled in her feet, and so had come safe to shore with her.

Dolly's tears fell fast over the mishap to her shoes, but she managed to wind up the line. When Dick's head appeared on the hill, Dolly went forth obediently on her mission, notwithstanding her own misfortune.

"Dick, I'm sorry! Here's your hook and line. I threw it into the place where the flag grows, and Doctor White says 'twas naughty, 'cause I shouldn't want you to have done so, if 'twas mine. He told me to get it and give it back to you, but you won't get the trout with it, will you, Dick? See! I've spoiled all my pretty boots, in the old black mud, a-finding of it," said Dolly, as Dick made no reply. She hoped to win him over by sympathy for her loss.

"It's just good enough for you. If I don't whip that doctor, if he's alive, when I get grown up, we'll see. I *wish* I could now."

"Dick! you look like 'old Peter'!" exclaimed Dolly, as Dick's face turned toward her, full freighted with anger.

Old Peter was an insane man, who had lived in the town of D——, and the ugliest-looking man that could be found, and to be likened unto him was almost more than Dick's human nature could endure. I am quite certain that Dolly would have received a severe blow, if it had not been for the black gig that stood at the gate.

With a revengeful look toward Dolly, Dick hurried in, with the parcel from the apothecary's.

Doctor White took it in silence, and proceeded to administer a portion of the contents to the invalid. After that, and a few words of cheer to Mrs. Jones, he mounted his gig, and the white horse bore him away across the river, to the widow's cottage.

Dolly had not yet told her story to Dick. She took off her boots and put them near the kitchen-fire to dry, and went in search of her brother. He was digging for angle-worms.

Divining his intent, Dolly felt an intense desire to stay him from the deed he was about to commit. But how could she do it? To tell her mother would only put off the evil hour a little longer. She knew he would embrace the first chance to disobey.

"O dear!" sighed Dolly. "What shall I do? Oh! I know. When Mr. Day wanted father to get better, he went right to God, and I guess He heard him, for father is getting better; so I'll go to Him too," and Dolly ran into the house, and up into her own room. She fell on her knees, and laid her arms on the stones of the chimney, and said: "O God! please don't let my brother Dick get the trout out of the well, please don't, for father told him not to, and now he's digging for worms in the garden. Don't let him find any worms, or, if he does, make the trout go fast asleep, so's they won't see any thing. Please God, *don't* let Dick do it."

As soon as Dolly's prayer was ended, she ran to the window to look out. Dick was gone. By the well she found him. The hook was baited, and cast in. With intense interest, Dolly watched the progress of events.

"You won't get any," she said.

"Great you know."

"Don't I, though! I've been up

stairs praying God to make the fish go to sleep, so's you can't catch 'em, and I know He will, for Mr. Day told father that God always gave people what they wanted very much, and asked for."

Dick held the hook and line only a minute longer. Then he resolutely drew it up, and walked away. Dolly's prayer made him afraid to **try to do evil.**

Chapter Ten.

DOLLY JONES had come into a new world, in her own very honest opinion. She was especially awed by the answer to the prayer that she had prayed, with her head laid upon the rough old stones of the chimney.

Dick tried his best to avoid Dolly and not to give her any chance to speak to him; but the little girl's love for her mother was stronger than Dick's purpose, and, ere many days, she told her story—the story of finding her mother in tears, because of the poverty that must surely come to them.

Dick stood still until Dolly had ended, and then he started off as fast as he could run toward the town.

Dolly called : " Dick ! Dick ! I haven't told you all, I didn't finish."

Dick paused to listen.

" Now what are you going to do ?" asked Dolly the instant she reached her brother.

"Do! what about? I'm just going to see what fun I can find."

" Oh ! how I wish I was a boy !"

" What for, pray ? You're ugly enough now, with your red hair."

Dolly's face was very dark for an instant, and then it brightened. " I will tell you what I'd do: I'd just go down into that big black place with the hot fires in it, where father worked, and I'd do his work, pull out the red hot strips of iron, like he does, and then when night comes get the money, and bring it right home to mother, to keep us all from going to the poorhouse. That's just what I'd do, if I was a man, or a boy either."

"I wouldn't then—it's too hard work."

"Work!" exclaimed Dolly. "Doesn't every body have to work that's good for any thing? Did you see Mrs. Day to work right in our kitchen? I never shall mind who sees me to work no more."

"I'm glad you like it. I thought you stopped me to tell something."

"Oh! I did," said Dolly. "And I want to, now; I want to tell you that if I was you, I'd go right down there and ask them to let me work on the iron bars. Do now, Dick, and I'll love you more'n I ever did."

Dick laughed a contemptuous little laugh, and said:

"Who cares for Dolly Jones's love?"

Poor Dolly! The tears gathered in her eyes, and overflowed them.

Dick had turned away and was walking on up the hill. With a sudden movement Dolly's hand doubled itself into a compact little weapon. She darted on and aimed it at Dick. It struck with force, for Dolly was strong in her anger.

Dick turned to retaliate; but at the instant, Dr. White's gig appeared in sight, and fear of the owner of it prevented his action.

Dolly was afraid that the Doctor had seen her strike her brother, and she turned, and ran with all speed toward home.

Dick kept on his way to the village, where he spent the day in search of some passing amusement. Play did not satisfy Dick on that day. Nothing interested him. He wandered from point to point, and late in the afternoon found himself near the mill where his father had been wont to labor for his bread.

"Dolly is a funny girl!" he thought. "Just to fancy Dick Jones slaving in there! I wonder if I could do it?" and prompted by his curiosity, Dick went in.

How black the place was! Huge black rafters, pointing far up into a blacker distance beyond, whose ending could not be seen. The faces of the men were black, and they were pouring molten metal.

How fiery the liquid stream looked, as it ran to and fro! The red-hot bars were being drawn into lengths that seemed ever increasing, and Dick stood still within the mill and watched the workmen.

Just out of the fiery furnace a mass of metal had been taken. Under a heavy roller it passed, and from thence was drawn out into a bar.

By some mischance, it slipped and fell. Ah! one of the workmen lies on the ground. He has fainted. He is a new hand, just come in to take Mr. Jones's place. He is not accustomed to the heat.

In a moment the fainting man is carried out into the pure air, and the bar of red-hot iron is caught up from the ground. It must not be left to cool, before it is drawn into proper proportions.

The workman looks around for some one to seize one end of it and draw it under the roller.

Through the din, he shouts to Dick: "Come here, and see if you can work as well as your father."

Dick approached the man, to hear what had been said to him, without the slightest idea of drawing the iron.

"Here, youngster! take hold of this, and see if you can pull it through. Quick now, before it cools, or we shall have to melt it over."

Dick seized the irons, and applied them to the hot bar. The roller went down, and the bar was drawn out one side.

"Catch it as it comes through!" shouted the man.

Dick obeyed, and imitated the movements of the man who had once drawn it through.

"Bravo!" shouted two or three workmen who had paused an instant, to note the effort of Dick.

Again and again the bar went under the heavy roller and was drawn out, and at length was laid down to rest with many others that had undergone a like process.

"Lazy Dick!" exclaimed some one, slapping Dick on his shoulder.

He turned to see who touched him. It was the master of the mill.

"Who ever saw you at work before?" he asked, as Dick's red face met his view.

"No one," answered Dick impulsively; "but—I like it," he slowly added.

"Not for long, but you may try it a little every day till you get used to it, and then when you like, you can become a workman. You may take your father's place yet."

Dick laughed. "I don't want to," he said.

"What will you do for a living?"

"I don't care," carelessly replied Dick; and glancing, as he spoke, at the entrance, he saw a friend passing by, and ran after him.

"What will become of that boy?" questioned the master of the mill of his own thoughts; but they gave to him no answer, and a few minutes later the owner of the property was deep in his cares, and Dick was forgotten.

But Dick had by no means forgotten himself. The boy was hungry, and hunger made him think of home.

He had wandered about on the hills during the morning, where a plentiful supply of strawberries had satisfied his then present need, but night was nearly come, and Dick turned his footsteps toward the valley where Rock House was.

Dolly had long been watching for her brother, for at home every thing had seemed to go wrong all the day.

Her father was irritable from continued pain. It had seemed as if Dick had never been of so much importance as on that day His mother had needed his services; the Doctor had required his presence; and his father had asked for him many times and grown very angry at his continued absence; and now night was casting heavy shadows toward the earth, and Dick was drawing near the place where Dolly waited.

She had climbed by the aid of a fence up among the low branches of a wild cherry-tree that looked as if it had been twisted to and fro by the storms of many years, and was looking eagerly forward over the road by which her brother must come.

He was close upon her before she saw him.

"Dick! Dick!" she called from the tree.

The boy stood perfectly still. He knew not from whence the voice came.

"Dick, wait one minute until I get down," she said.

"Pray, where on earth are you?"

"Up here, in the tree, waiting for you."

"Get down then, quick, I'm just starving. I say, what have you got to eat at home?"

"Dick, won't you help me? It's too far to jump; I'm afraid!"

"Girls haven't any business in trees; get down the way you went up!" and without waiting an instant or giving the least aid to his sister, Dick Jones moved off.

Dolly saw him going, and believed there was no way to reach the ground except by the "jump" she so much dreaded; so, gathering carefully the folds of the dress that Lulu Day had given her in her hands, she tried it.

Poor Dolly was unfortunate; a fold of her dress, despite the care she had taken, caught in a gnarled branch and impeded her fall. The dress was torn, and Dolly's face and hands were bruised and bleeding when she reached home. Tears were falling rapidly down her face, for the wounds gave her quick, smarting pains as she entered the house.

"Hallo! what's the matter?" cried Dick, and a momentary consciousness of his own baseness entered Dick Jones's mind, as he saw Dolly's distress.

"Oh! I wish, I wish you wasn't my brother; I wish Albert Elder was my brother," sobbed Dolly, wringing her smarting hands.

"You do, do you? *May be* Albert Elder wouldn't want *you* for a sister. I'll swap! I'd much rather take Fanny Elder, any day."

"What is this, what is the matter, Dolly?" questioned Mrs. Jones, who at the instant entered the kitchen from her husband's room.

"I'll tell you, mother," spoke up Dick. "Dolly's been climbing trees, and has got punished for it; it's just right. Is there any pie, mother?"

For once in her life, Mrs. Jones befriended Dolly. She took no notice of Dick's question regarding pie, but proceeded to bathe Dolly's bruises in warm water, and to ask her kindly how she came to fall. But Dolly could only sob and cry, and answer that she would " tell some time all about it."

The day had been full of trials to Mrs. Jones. She felt ready to sink under them. Mr. Jones was just in the condition that required the utmost care, and constant attention; and since the early morning his wife had not obtained one moment of rest.

The sobs and tears of Dolly were the crowning trial of the day, and no sooner were the bleeding bruises bathed and made comfortable, than Mrs. Jones was ready to cry with her child. She stood in the large old kitchen, that she had taken great trouble to keep neat, since the advent of Mrs. Day, with her hands pressed tightly on her head, trying to keep back the tide of feeling, when Dick emerged from the pantry, with his hands filled with whatever of food he had been able to find.

"It's real good, this pie," said Dick. "Where did it come from?"

"O Dick! you've taken it *all!*" exclaimed Dolly. "We've been saving it for tea, so's we could eat it together — mother, and you and I."

"I'm hungry; haven't had one bite of dinner," replied Dick, his large mouth opening wider than ever, and the pie disappearing rapidly.

"Dick, put that down, now; it was sent here to day, expressly for Dolly, and she has been waiting to share it with you."

"Well, I declare, I never heard the like—a whole pie sent to Dolly Jones! Who did it, pray?" and, taking an additional morsel, Dick deposited the remains of what had been a pie, on the table. Dolly's pie! that had been such a pleasure to look at all day, and to think of, as a surprise to her brother.

Dolly was too indignant to weep any more, even over her own bruises.

Dick turned to leave the room. He opened the door, and upon the stone step stood Mrs. Day.

Dolly sprang forward instinctively, to cover the mutilated pie, lest it should meet the eyes of the minister's wife, but all too late; that lady was in the room.

"Why, Dolly!" she said, "what was the matter with my pie—was it not nice? and what has happened to you?"

Dolly's face flushed crimson, her auburn eyes were on the floor; she could not answer Mrs. Day.

Only that morning she would have spoken at once, and said, "My bad brother, Dick, stole it out of the pantry, and was eating it up, when mother stopped him," but now, she could not, and not knowing what to say, she said nothing.

"Dolly has been saving her pie very carefully, to share with her brother at tea, but he came home and took it.

Dolly had a fall from a tree," explained Mrs. Jones.

Mrs. Day turned to look for Dick. He was out of sight.

"I was waiting to tell him I'd got it, and that you sent it," said Dolly.

"Well, never mind, you shall have another one," kindly said Mrs. Day, and then she inquired after Mr. Jones, and went in and spoke gentle, cheering words to him, of his hoped for recovery, and the future life that she trusted he would make better and brighter under the new light that had come into his soul.

A few moments, and the visit of the minister's wife was ended. It was a very little thing, but her words and her presence had wrought out of the darkness, light and gladness that diffused themselves through the house, and reached up into Dolly's airy sleeping-room, where that little girl had gone to exchange her torn dress for the one that so lately had been dripping from her accidental fall with the pail of water.

Dolly stood at the window, and looked out upon the road, in the soft summer twilight, and saw the kind lady go over it, and pass out of sight. Dolly's auburn eyes grew strangely soft, as a mist crept into them, and her little bruised hands were softly laid on the rough stones of the chimney that went up through her room, and her flushed face found a moment's rest on her hands, and her little heart went up past the chimney, and the roof and the sky, and the stars—went up to the kind Father of heaven and earth, with a little song of thanksgiving. Only the angel who heard it, could tell the words of Dolly's song; it was not lisped in language of the lips.

When Dolly left her place of prayer she had almost forgotten her bruises, some healing balm had surely been poured into them; for when her mother called her, she went down and answered Dick's question regarding the pie, with a smile.

Now, Dick was fully prepared for a display of temper on Dolly's part, and he framed his question so as to exasperate the child as much as he could.

When he saw the sweet smile on her face, and listened to the words,

"Mrs. Day sent it to me, but I don't mind any thing about it; you may eat the rest if you want it, I know you must be hungry, going all day without your dinner," he stood perfectly unable to understand Dolly.

"Why! what's come over you?" he asked, as his sister returned from the pantry, bearing the remains of the pie in her hands, and placed it before him.

"I'm going to try and be good, to be just as much like Christ Jesus, as I can," simply said Dolly, and for an instant, the freckled face changed, in Dick's imagination, to one of beauty.

But Dick's eyes wandered to the remains of his late feast, and in an instant he had seized it, and not caring that his mother should see him devouring Dolly's share, he made good his escape.

Dick's thoughts under the pear-tree, where he stood out of sight of the house, were a marvel to himself.

"I don' know, now, as I would change off Dolly for Fanny. I don't believe she'd give me the whole of her pie, and I don't believe she'd keep things as Dolly does, and never tell. I wonder what's become of Albert Elder and his piety. These good folks an't so much better than other folks," and in instant Dick's thoughts ran back to the old mill, and the few minutes of honest labor that he had performed there that afternoon.

He ran into the house and shouted: "Dolly! Dolly! come here, I've something to tell you."

Now Dick's voice was unusually pleasant, and Dolly obeyed the summons with alacrity.

"I've been to work in the mill, to-day," said Dick.

"O Dick! how glad I am. I'd given you the whole of that in a minute, if I'd only known; why didn't you tell?"

"'Cause you didn't give me time; and, Dolly, I am kind o' sorry I didn't help you down out of the tree," he added, noticing how badly her hands were scratched.

"Never mind that now. You don't know how glad I am; I don't want to be a boy, a bit now, 'cause you can work. Mother's been counting up father's money to-day, and there an't but just five pieces of silver, and they an't very big neither, and when that's gone she says she don't know what we can do; do you, Dick?"

Alas! Dick Jones was not born a hero, or he would have given the little being beside him, then and there, words of encouragement and brave promises, to be more bravely fulfilled, of care for her always. But he did not; he only toyed with the flowers, and thought it would be "awful to work all day long in the black mill, drawing to and fro bars of hot iron."

"Dick, are you going to work tomorrow?" she timidly asked, as he gave no sign of having heard her.

"I'm going fishing to-morrow," carelessly said Dick.

What a shadow the words brought

over Dolly Jones! Even Dick's heart would have felt it, had his eyes watched it stealing over her face.

There came a time when Mr. Jones could be left a few minutes in safety, and Mrs. Jones went up to Dolly's room. That little girl had gone to bed. The full moon shone in and made the room everywhere clearly visible.

It was very unusual for Mrs. Jones to look especially after Dolly's comfort, but she did on that night.

"Dolly," she said, sitting down on the side of her bed, "tell me about your fall to-day; I wish to know how it happened."

Dolly sighed, and began her story: "You know, mother, the day you cried because father was hurt and couldn't earn any money?"

"Yes, Dolly," said Mrs. Jones, for Dolly paused, as if waiting for an answer.

"Well, then, when I saw you, I wanted to do something to keep us all from going to the poor-house, and I thought if I was a man I could, and so I wanted to be one, 'cause you know little girls can't do much; they don't earn money. Well, when Dick came home I went to tell him how you'd been crying and to ask him if he wouldn't do some work to buy us things to eat, and some how it all got wrong." Dolly was about to say that "Dick was ugly and she couldn't tell him," but the words were staid in time, and she went on: "Then, mother, I got angry with Dick and hid his fish-hook and line in the swamp, and spoiled my pretty shoes trying to find it; and some how, I never could get a chance to tell Dick until this morning. I ran up the road and he waited to hear me; I told him that if he would only go and work in the mill I'd love him more'n ever I did."

Here Dolly came to a pause.

"Well, what then, Dolly?"

The tone was encouraging.

"Then, mother, he said: '*Who cares for Dolly Jones's love?*' Don't *you*, mother? Don't you care for my love, if I am ugly and have got red hair and big freckles on my face? I love you, mother," and the tears came and fell down on Dolly's pillow for a moment, and then the freckled face and the red hair were at rest on her mother's heart, and Dolly received more kisses than she had in many days, and the firm assurance, that, at least, one person in the world cared for Dolly Jones's love.

"Mother, I struck him! I struck Dick just as hard as I could, I was so mad at him for saying that; and just as soon as I struck him I looked up and I saw Dr. White coming, and I was afraid and ran home. Dr. White didn't see me at all, mother; but I'll tell you who did. He was coming 'cross lots; he'd been up somewhere for his Aunt Hannah, to get something for her, and he saw me strike Dick and then run home. I didn't see him, though; but when the doctor was in here with father and you, and I was hiding in the kitchen for fear he'd see me, somebody gave a little bit of a knock on the door, and I opened it and Albert Elder stood right there, and he whispered almost, and told me he wanted to tell me something if I'd just come out by the well. And, mother, you couldn't guess what he told me! 'Twas all about seeing me strike Dick, and how sorry he was. And then he told me that I must never strike Dick, but the more he treated me bad, the kinder I must be to him He told me all about Christ Jesus and how much He loves every body, and I asked him 'Who told him about it?' and he said Mr. Day told him, and that he used to be very unhappy; but now, trying to do right made him feel better. And then I asked him if Christ Jesus would care as much about me as if I had pretty hair like Lulu Day, and hadn't any freckles on my face, and wore nice clothes. And he said that Christ didn't stop to see if we had red or black or white hair; that He looked right down through, to see if he could find any love in our hearts, and the more we loved Him the more He would love us. You can't think, mother, how happy it made me feel to think *somebody* would love me. You love Dick, and I love you and father too; but you see, I hadn't a single body to love me; had I, mother?"

The question went home with a

sudden pain to Mrs. Jones's heart. Conscience told her that she had not given of her heart's strong love to Dolly, the plain little girl who had lived in her home, but that it had been concentrated on Dick, the handsome, bright, wicked boy, who had never given her much cause for joy, but abundance of trouble.

She gathered Dolly in her arms and assured her that henceforth she should have a mother's love, and Dolly went to sleep with a bright hope of happy days to come.

Chapter Eleven.

THE days and the weeks and the months sped on, each keeping its appointed round.

Albert Elder held fast to the new hope that had entered into his life— and it never failed him.

Mrs. Elder's recovery was but in part. She could never take up again all the cares of the family, that she had so suddenly laid down, but she was able to resume many of the duties of her life.

With abundant joy, she witnessed the change in Albert, and saw him day by day growing into a consistent Christian life.

Upon Aunt Hannah the change worked a wonderful influence. She had never considered children any thing more than a necessary trouble, to be gotten on with as best one might until they arrived at wisdom's years; but now, at her age, to have all the ideas of her life changed as Albert Elder was changing them, proved almost more than she could bear.

To see him enduring with a smile her severest reproofs, and returning her cross words with acts of thoughtful kindness; to feel that he was trying to please her; to witness his devotion to his mother, and his gentle guidance of Fanny, his tenderness for her fears, and patience with her slow mind in its growth, proved more than Aunt Hannah's stoicism could withstand

One day, it was in the winter, and the weather had been terribly severe for more than a week, a swift messenger arrived from Aunt Hannah's home, to summon her thither, for her father was dying.

"O dear! what shall I do? I can't leave you, and I must go!" she said, after the first weight of the news had fallen upon her.

Mrs. Elder was not strong enough to be left, and there was no one to stay with her. The messenger waited to convey Aunt Hannah Elder to her father.

"Aunt Hannah!" said Albert, "you

When that was ended, she prayed: "Dear Father up in heaven, my aunt Hannah has come here to day, because my mother is sick. I don't love her one bit. She's cross, and she don't love me a bit more'n I love her. Won't you please to make mother get up off of the bed again, so's she can go back to grandfather's house, where the little children are all growed up so's she can't strike 'em? Please, God, bless my mother and my brother, and make him a good boy, so's he won't run off any more, and leave mother to cry when Dick Jones comes and tells what a bad boy he's been. Don't let him pull my hair any more. Amen."

"There! you see I had to pray just what was in my heart to pray, and you mustn't be cross at me," said Fanny, rising up and standing just in the window-frame of moonlight, that lay across the carpet. Albert caught the little white figure in his arms, kissed it with a love in his heart that never had been there before, and then he tossed it as high as he could, and it fell right into the midst of the best feather-bed in the guest-chamber. Just as he did so, a little noise was heard down the stairway.

Aunt Hannah had deemed it her duty to look after Fanny, and to see that she was properly committed to the angel of sleep for the night. To that end she had, in her carpet slippers, softly ascended the stair-case, just in time to hear Fanny's prayer.

you will know what makes you think boys are different."

It was many hours ere Aunt Hannah had the opportunity to read Albert's note, for she reached home in the hour of her father's release from earth.

When she opened the folded paper, she found these words there written:

DEAR AUNT HANNAH: I was a very bad, wicked boy until Mr. Day told me how to live better; told me to go to God with all my sins and tell Him about them, and to ask Him to forgive them for Jesus' sake.

It isn't because I am good; only God has made me kinder to you and to every body; and I don't want to take the credit for what God has done, and made me do.

ALBERT.

Chapter Twelve.

YEARS have passed **away** since the night on which Dolly Jones felt the assurance of her mother's love; since the time when Aunt Hannah went to her home through the hours of the night, to find her father on the verge between the life that we know and the life that we know not.

Mr. Jones recovered in due time, and the repentance that seemed so sincere when he lay, as he believed on the bed of death, proved in his after-life, to have been true sorrow for sin. He fought bravely with his old temptations, that had not wholly lost their power, as he lay shut out from the world in his own house, and so fighting, was enabled to overcome them. Mrs. Jones's silent prayers were answered for her husband, and her heart would have been filled with joy, but for Dick. Nothing seemed to make any lasting impression on him. He went to the iron-mill and tried to work; but he felt no strong purpose stirring within him, and he soon grew weary of labor, and returned to his old habits and mode of life.

Mrs. Elder lived a few years, and died in the hope of a blest immortality; died with words of blessing on her lips—blessing Albert for his tender love that had made life a joy to her.

Albert and Fanny were alone. Aunt Hannah left to her dear nephew, Albert Elder, all her earthly possessions, when the angel of death called her to go forth with him—" because through him she had learned the lesson of love." Thus said the quaint will that was found after her departure from earth.

The month of May came again with blossoms of promise smiling out from the tears of April that had softened the frozen heart of earth, causing it to spring forth in joy, and so all the land was decked in glory.

Birmingham has grown into a goodly town. The Rock House has passed away. Not "one stone upon another," is left of the rough chimney that had been Dolly Jones's altar of prayer The house became too old to be inhabited. Mr. Jones became a prominent workman, and was able to live in a better house. Dolly alone wept at its destruction. She watched the workmen take down the building. Her jealous eyes viewed every stone of the chimney as it was dislodged from its long resting-place; but they were fastened upon one that the young girl was determined to possess. It was that one, on which, leaning, she had offered up her first *heart-felt* prayer that God would not let Dick catch the fish.

For her sake, although knowing nothing of its sacredness, the rough workmen lifted it down gently and carried it for her to her new home. Dolly guards it as her dearest earthly treasure. God *is* everywhere; but in her heart of hearts, He seems nearer to her when she kneels to pray, with her head upon this altar-stone.

In the soft May air, a young woman approaches the stone. It is hidden from public view by a thicket of evergreens. The face that looks through the boughs seeking for it, is a very sweet face, clustered around with curls of auburn hue. It is Dolly Jones. She is dressed for a journey, evidently, and seems in haste. The thicket of evergreens is parted, and she is shut in. Human eyes can not follow her there, as she kneels on the sod and lays her sweet young face, with its wealth of tenderness and love, on the rough old stone, and prays to God a prayer from the very depth of her heart; prays that a blessing may rest upon her journey, and that its object may be crowned with success.

All the valley is green, and the waters of the Housatonic and the Naugatuck flow together, in joy that their long journey is so near its haven, the sea, as Dolly crosses from the new village of Birmingham to the old town of Derby.

Should you think Dolly's face would look bright or glad, when it is turned toward a prison? But it does. It is a face that nothing can long dim, for, seeing past all things that cloud us here, it looks forward to the heavenly city, and from afar the amber light rests upon it.

Dolly meets friends at the railroad station, who are ready to go with her on her sad errand.

Theodore Day is there, and Lulu, who is as lovely as ever in Dolly's eyes; and at the last moment, Albert Elder's manly face is seen, just in time to catch the waiting train.

The prison is large and strong, and Dolly shudders as its stone walls are before her. As the ponderous gates are parted to admit her, and close with a solid sound, shutting her in, she shudders still more, and clings for an instant to the arm that supports her.

"If you please, Albert, I would rather see Dick alone, just at the first, you know, and then you may all come in," whispered Dolly, and the request was granted.

Alone with the conductor Dolly went. The cell-door was opened, and in a moment more, Dolly Jones was locked in with her brother Dick.

The criminal looked up.

"Dolly! Dolly Jones! Have you come to see me here?" exclaimed the man, rising from the corner where he had long been crouching in gloomy inaction.

"Yes, Dick, for you *are* my brother, and *I love you*," said Dolly, and the sweet young face looked up into that of the condemned man, and words were spoken whose power went through all the past, straight home to Dick's heart. We know not what

they were. We only know that the
prayer that went up from the little
altar of stone in the thicket of evergreens, found its answer in the cell
where Dick Jones was working out the
punishment due for crime committed
against his country's laws.

"I'll carry home your promise to
comfort mother's heart," said Dolly, at
the last.

"Dolly," said Dick, "I would not
change you for all the sisters in Connecticut. You are brave, and *beautiful!*" added Dick, and his eyes lingered lovingly on Dolly's face, until it
was shut out by the strong door of
his cell that closed behind her.

"Mother! mother!" said Dolly, the
instant she reached home, " Dick has
a heart; I've found it at last. And

oh! I am so thankful it is seeking for God's love."

The tears of mother and daughter fell together over the promise that the words gave, a promise that was fulfilled.

Dick's prison-life was not in vain. He said, not long ago: "It was Dolly's kindness and love that saved me; it even found me in prison and visited me." But, as Albert Elder had done, Dolly disclaimed the work, and gave the glory to the Heart of Love that always waits and watches for returning children.

The night that Dick came home, Dolly was lost from human view. They searched for her to tell the glad tidings: "Dick is come home!"

Dolly knew that he was near, Albert

Elder had brought to her in secret the glad tidings, and Dolly had gone to her altar of stone to offer up a song of thanksgiving.

www.ingramcontent.com/pod-product-compliance
Lightning Source LLC
Chambersburg PA
CBHW032205230426
43672CB00011B/2516